I0467194

Invest With A Genius.
By
Michael Levy

Now is the time to Plant Super Seeds of prosperity in the mind, body and soul. As soon as we master how to cultivate them, they will display the succulent fruits of a successful life. We will Supersede our wildest expectations with true prosperity.

In our life long journey, we will encounter many obstruction of negativity that hinder our resolve and fortitude. Michael's wisdom informs us that all obstacle in life are made to jump over and as soon as we obtain the Supervision of enlightened foresight, we gain:

Super — Vision.

CONTENTS PAGE.

Copyright 2002 by point of Life Inc.

All rights reserved.

No part of this publication may be reproduced or transmitted in any form or by any means ,electronic, mechanical, including photocopy, recording, or any information storage and retrieval system, without permission in writing from the publisher.

Requests for permission to make copies of any part of the work should be made to Permission Dept; Point of Life Inc, PO Box 3507, Boynton Beach, FL 33424 or contact us on the web at www.pointoflife.com email mikmikl@aol.com
"http://www.pointoflife.com."

The opinions expressed in this book are those of the author. He is not medically qualified and any opinion regarding investments, and health are based on his life experiences. Readers should consult a medical professional before making any changes to medication, exercise regimens, diet or any heath related issues. Investments should be made with careful decisions and this book is meant as a guide only and no investments should be made, solely on the information in this book.

First printing January   2002

ISBN **0-9668069-4-8.**
Printed in the United States of America

Acknowledgments.

I am very grateful to Ruth and Bev at Silverleaf designs for all

their kind support in keeping my web site;
www.pointoflife.com up and running for the past two years

I thank my wife Margaret for all her love and kind support.

I desire to express my gratitude to all the past philosophers and
sages who's quotes I have used in this book.

Since everything is supplied by spirit, on behalf of all humans
on planet earth, I would like to thank the intelligent energies of
the universe. These forces infuse all life with intelligence and
feed all humankind with the information to be able to live in
Love & Joy.

I would also like to thank you the reader, for taking the time to
read and digest this book.

About The Author Michael Levy

Michael Levy was born in Manchester England on the 6th of
March 1945. The second world war was drawing to a close and
folks were just beginning to pick up the remnants of five hard
years of conflict.

Michael recalls the early days of his childhood; they were
exciting times. Every day was an adventure on the streets of the

inner city community. Nobody had any spare money. Even candy was on ration until 1950 but nobody ever informed Michael he was poor. He just knew there were only so many hours in each day and he was here to enjoy them. He was a little mischievous in a kindly way and brought lots of Joy into many peoples lives. He always went around with a big smile on his face and nobody was able to wipe it away.

He left school at sixteen and meandered through a few jobs until he hit the tender age of nineteen. He married, and with a child on the way, went to work on the street markets with $60 worth of cloth remnants. It was hard to get a stall so he would put a sheet on the floor and sell his textiles from the sidewalk. He truly started from the ground and could only move upwards.

By the time Michael reached twenty eight he had build up a highly successful wholesale textile corporation. Whilst continuing to run his textile business Michael started to invest in commercial property in a run down area in the city of Manchester. This was against the advice of associates and professionals. It turned out to be a great move . The area is now thriving and the center of club life in the North West of England.

All this time Michael was investing in the stock market very successfully. He has been an investor/trader for thirty- six years and has performed as a good juggler with Balls. He also traded Commodities for sixteen years and found the experience very enlightening.
His prowess and ability as a businessman and stock market wizard has never been questioned and now you have a chance to learn Michael secrets.

Michael retired a very successful businessman in 1992. It took six years of deep though and meditation before he could explain the source of his success. The smile has never left Michael face and he learnt it is the *Joy of Life* that is the force that gives him a prosperous life. In 1998 Michael wrote his first book *"What is The Point"* in only ten days. Quickly followed by *"Minds of Blue Souls of Gold"* and *"Enjoy Yourself It's Later Than ."* He had left school at sixteen and had never read a worthwhile book or even written many letters up to the juncture of writing his first book..

The guiding force has always been the Spirit of the Universe. Michael has no particular religious affiliations, but has always been aware God will show him the way. He has never asked for favors from God or even had time to pray. But he is a great listener and as God knows every thought in his head Michael knew it was best to listen in silence and allow his subconscious mind to receive Spirits wisdom.

The reason we all exist on earth is to enjoy our time on earth. This simple philosophy is so hard for the intellect to understand. Michael will continue to reach out into a, negative, misguided world and will slowly touch the hearts, minds and Souls of all folks, for ALL folks deserve to be Happy, Healthy and Wealthy.

The Best is Yet To Come. In Michael's words " Many people talk about success but only a few really live it." This book will shine the light so you may find the doorway to Prosperity.

Michael Levy is the author of "What is the Point." "Minds of Blue Souls of Gold." "Enjoy Yourself It's Later Than You Think".
His Articles and Poems are now published on over 1000 web sites, journals and magazines. His latest story has been published in "Chicken Soup for the Jewish Soul" He has appeared on hundreds of radio programs, TV in the U K and USA and was a recent guest on the Howard Stern Show. He is

a keynote guest speaker on Finance, Health and Inspiration

Kites rise highest against the wind - not with it. - Winston Churchill

****

When -Becomes- The Now By Michael Levy

When we can endure to attend the veracity we've voiced,
Warped by scallywags and scoundrels to produce a snare for the gullible,
When we preserve the energy of Love & Joy in all the senses,
With only the resolve which tells of powers beyond mortal frames.

Even though we can observe our foremost thoughts of truth,
Others my be evading their veracities and denouncing us;
Still in all the turmoil we must entrust ourselves with faith,
For if we will remain with truth, we'll never pale by remaining.

As long as we aspire outside life's illusions, becoming our own wizard,
When we can gather ourselves with serenity, in jubilation or catastrophe,
And handle these two deceivers just as a parallel of equals
With a solid foundation that ministers to the test of time,

When we will assemble a mountain of all our prosperity and comfort,
And then when jeopardy encroaches, chance the outcome?
Defeat becomes the result, now can we establish a new dawn?
In quietude pursue new horizons with no murmur of complaint.

When the lover or the foe cannot shadow the real being within
When the many sing our song, but not for long,
When we will converse with assemblies and they oppose our excellence,

When we will preserve great strength when all seems lost,

When we will embrace a higher reality in an untruthful
conditioned world,
When we can live with detachment of ego and fly with eagles,
Only then will our shackles release, as the breeze of memories set
sail,

When-becomes The Now;
On incessant cosmic seas, we find true authenticity.

PREFACE.

There is a formula for true success that cannot fail. Each person
embodies a genius with a wealth of information, that can locate
true prosperity. Successful living means an abundance in
health, wealth and Joy.

Money is not a means to success, it merely is a instrument of
exchange that can bring a certain amount of security. The stock
markets seems to be the 'game' folks like to play the most at
this time in our history. This book will enlighten the weary
investor of various methods and techniques that will change
their lives.

The stock markets of today are comparable to a zoo with no
intelligent keepers. The gyrations are enough to make the
strongest animals 'sick to death.' Indeed many illnesses will
arise from all the stress and worry generated by fear and greed
over the past few years.

When we peer behind the scenes on the floor of the exchanges,
we will run into charging bulls, squeezing bears and a few

grazing stags. Many sheep come along to the fountain of plenty wanting their 'fair share,' only to be slaughtered by their ignorance of how it all functions. The sheep that survive, live with a mind that contains worries and anxieties.

Quietly, the piggies continue to feed on greed, whilst the little lemmings live in fear, just waiting to be shoved off a high priced stock. The young lion and tiger brokers stalk their prey with free dinners and seminars. Little do the poor little lambs realize they will be the main course at the stock brokers banquet at a 'futures' date.

The only options for many is Hobson's choice. If they don't invest they believe they are missing the Ark. If they do invest their stocks sink. Who is the captain of the boat? Who is the lookout? And who becomes the weakest link?

A feast of plenty continues for the brokers as long as their golden geese keep laying their investment eggs. Yes, the menagerie of animals ravenous for quick profits, boosts the pockets of those who manipulate the markets with analysts comments.

Some analysts are quite unique animals. They live in a world of fantasy and imagine a companies stock price can go to infinite heights. A Realistic P/E value is not to be considered of any use. Well, that is until the fantasy bubble bursts. Then they will disown the company and tell folks to sell, once the stock starts to hit rock bottom. Only now does the P/E ratio matter.

This analyst predator is a great decoy that brings in millions of dollars in commission to the brokers. Buy and Sell recommendations keep the roller coaster running and all the sheep have the thrill of losing their hard earned money.

The SEC (securities and exchange commission) recently

published a communication, warning investors Not to rely solely on stock analysts reports. Talk about closing the door after the horse has bolted. Where were they in 1999 when the market was going into orbit?

It is about time we came out from the cages of ignorance? We need to start taking responsibility for our actions "forewarned is forearmed." Once we can begin to understand the motors that drive the markets we will be able to steer a more sustainable, profitable course.

If we want to sail to success, we have to locate our inner captain. We will then have the awareness to comprehend how to invest wisely and without anxiety. We will recognize the genius that has been silently within us all the time we have been on planet Earth. We will arrive at a point where we find our true self. We can then commence on our quest for prosperity as we Invest with a Genius.
****

To a developed intellectual mind "The TRUTH" is often rejected at first, then embraced later. The knack is to discover it sooner, rather than later. M. L.

A student will always be a student until he/she becomes a master of the mind. M. L.

Establishing A Connecting To The Genius.

There is a perfect inflow and outflow of resources. When we go with the flow we gain assets and when we go against the flow we lose wealth. Once we begin to understand our connection to universal wisdom, we will achieve many wondrous accomplishments cultivated by the universal deeds of limitless supply. These actions cannot be hampered, restricted or held back in any way, other than the domination of our own thoughts.

We are part of an endless supply of universal energy that can magnetize our desires by the action of our thoughts. These thoughts go beyond status, past accounts of happenings and past experiences. To be able to benefit from the fertile flawlessness that naturally abounds, it is a necessity to erase any remains of past experiences of guilt, fear, and feelings of being "an unlucky person."

No mortal being or company has any special monopoly on any supply or demand that we cannot trade in. To believe we are inferior because someone or some organization has more money or power are self defeating thoughts. These kind of thoughts will frustrate us before we begin to accomplish our coveted lifestyle. False opinions spring from a mistaken belief in our counterfeit powers and possessions. Once we believe there is a demand to compete with these inaccurate powers, we become manipulated by them.

We then try to manipulate others with catastrophic results for our credibility. Clarity of mind, without personal preconceived, conditioned, "value judgments" is essential for accomplishing our wishes and desires. The *Creative Universal Force* is sufficient unto itself, to grant us a contented lifestyle.

There are many secrets of the soul we will learn from this enlightening book. We are going to learn how to invest in the stock market without anxiety. We will learn about our most precious assets and how we spend them wisely. We will find the secrets of how we can live like a millionaire. A serving of health and wellness wisdom will be included for good measure. Most of all we will learn to enjoy each second of each day and grow the magnificence of our pure potential.

Many pitfalls await the unaware investor. Once we know how to invest our money wisely, we will gain more assets but it does not end there. Many folks have gained wealth only to lose it at a later date. We are going to discover who it is locked away inside us, who recognizes all the answers to life's conundrum. As we journey into the wise thoughts of our protector, we will begin to find our authentic self. The true genius will reveal-true solutions- to many of life's un-ponderable riddles. The magic of an inspirational, prosperous life is now in our grasp. As we turn the first page, we are on the path to a flourishing life.

What lies behind us and what lies before us are tiny matters compared to what lies within us." Ralph Waldo Emerson

Market Overview.
The one thing that is certain is the fact all stock markets are uncertain. The markets are chancy, dangerous, daring and

adventurous. Today, many people exhibit a casino type mentality. The stock market spins on a wheel of fortune.

When it comes to knowing which direction the market is heading we need to comprehend there are NO experts. No one really knows it's direction. Using only logic and reasoning will be a quick way of going broke. Just like a roulette wheel, round and round it goes, where it stops no one knows.

The word sucker was used in 1929 crash because folks were sucked into the market by greed. When the greed became to much, the fear took over and down came the Dow, suckers and all. But it did not start in 1929. There have been many instances before that date where folks have lost all their money by unsound, unwise, investing techniques.

If we go all the way back to the early seventeenth century in Holland, folks got all heated up by flower power. The tulip bulb became the golden goose of the era. The price of one bulb became astronomical. It grew out of it's petals. Then one fine day the bottom fell out of the Tulip mania and the folks went home broke. At least they had some pretty flowers to display.

Since the 1929 crash, there have been many ups and downs but if we would have invested in the original Dow Jones stocks, we would be left with many valueless pieces of paper. We would be owning pieces of paper representing companies that went out of business many years ago. Although the index has gone up substantially, we still have to be aware of the correct stocks to buy. Timing when to buy and sell is imperative to wise investing and we will be discussing that in later chapters.

In 1950 the Dow index was just 201. In 1969 the Dow Jones was trading at 1000. In 1982 the Dow Jones was still trading at 1000. Thirteen years absent of any growth in the index, but there was still money to be made by the wise investor.

Knowing the psychology of the stock market and the philosophy to find substantial gains is not easy for most people. If it were, everyone would become millionaires but the facts tell a different story.

Since March 2000 the stock markets have been on a downward spiral. The index's do not show the true carnage that has transpired. Many hi tech stocks are down by more than ninety percent. Even the generals such as; Microsoft, Intel, Sun, Oracle, Cisco and numerous others are down by over sixty percent.
This has been the worst crash of all time in value terms. At one point just one stock; Cisco, had lost four hundred billion dollars in market value. Many folks have lost their hard earned money in many similar hi tech stocks.

There is no doubt the manufacturing sector went into recession in 2000 and the overcapacity in inventory takes a long while to work though the system. The big problem for hi tech companies is if they don't sell there products quickly they become almost worthless. Most technology products are now valued as commodities with a short shelf life. How long a slump lasts is anyone's guess but one thing is for sure. It will be a very long while before the Nasdaq index hits 5000 again.

At the start of 2001 the federal reserve began to cut interest rates. At the same time a new president was elected. Tax cuts and an economic stimulus package came into effect and more will no doubt follow. These types of measures usually stimulate a soft economy and allow certain stocks to advance.

There are constantly many opportunities opening up before us to earn money, no matter what sectors are suffering.
The utilities and energy sectors had a good run in 2000 and the first few months of 2001, then they reversed. The housing sector has been a good investment area in 2001 whilst most

drug stocks just tread water. This is a small example of how our awareness must be receptive to changing circumstances.

Many market bottoms are made when many analysts cut their expectations. This usually happens when stocks are trading at yearly lows and many sell signals are given out by financial "*Experts*". At the beginning of 2000 the analyst's told us "It is different this time. We are in a new age, a new paradigm." Many 'Buy' recommendations were being made left, right and center, on many stocks with unsustainable, ludicrous values.

The next time an 'expert' gives a buy rating on a stock that is trading on it's yearly high, with a ridiculous valuation, question it's validity? This expertise spreads and when taxi drivers and barbers become stock picking experts, understand it is time to head for the exit doors.
So let's get started with a few of the basics, on how we can invest in the stock market without anxiety. We will grant ourselves the distinction to become acquainted with the genius that will light our pathway to Riches beyond belief.
"An invasion of armies can be resisted, but not an idea whose time has come." Victor Hugo
No 1 Nothing is written in Stone.

All the rules are made to be broken even golden one's. Whatever rules there are in investing, there are always times when they do not count. We need to always keep an open mind and be able to change direction at a moment's notice.

If we only follow advise from our past memories that have been programmed into our memory banks, we could go bankrupt. We will not be able to go with the constantly changing flow. We can equate our thoughts to the wind. It is constantly changing direction. When it blows in bad weather, we put on warmer clothing. In warm weather, we wear light clothing. Our mind must learn adapt to conditions of the moment. Passed moments don't count. Future one's have not arrived so we should acclimatize ourselves to the present situations with our inner geniuses foresight.

The more aware we become of world news, company events and balance sheets, the more likely we are to make the correct decisions. The more correct decisions we make, the richer we will become. After all is said and done, the reason we are buying stocks, is simply to make money. It is not an ego thing, where we have to protect our pride. It requires wisdom to constantly beat the street. A stock is just a piece of paper with words scribbled on it. It only holds a value as long as a number of people trust in its value. Once its credibility collapses so does its value. All stocks hold risk.

It is essential to define our risk tolerance and never exceed it. The more money we have, the less gambles should be to taken. We should compose a wish list of desires and aspirations and a time horizon to achieve the goals. The younger we are the more risk tolerance we can assume.

Older folks need a steady income and few risky investments. Treasury bills, tax free municipals and maybe a few corporate bonds should make up the bulk of their investment portfolio. Even a few convertible bonds can be a boost. The older we are the fewer our ventures into perilous monetary undertakings. Therefore, this means we should put less of our capital into the stock markets. That being said, when a money market account or C D only yields two percent we need to look at other alternatives. We should always remember, the bigger the return, the greater the danger of losses.

We have to learn to balance risk with the potential rewards. If a stock is trading at it's yearly high and is being tipped all over the place, we have to ask how much more has it left in it's price to advance. It is far better to buy an unglamourous out of favor stock, that has the potential to go up ten or twenty percent in a rebound from being oversold, than a darling that everyone "*loves*" and it is overpriced.

When we look at an out of favor sector we want to find the best companies in that sector, which are selling at the lowest P/E ratio's. Big rewards come from overlooked and misunderstood companies. Many times the markets are slow to recognize mis_priced, undervalued stocks.

The number one enemy of the stock markets is inflation and it is important to keep a keen eye on the lookout for any signs of this foe. When an economy picks up its pace and demand exceeds supply, inflation rears it's ugly head and scares all the investors away. Interest rates start to climb and companies stop their spending because it becomes too costly to borrow money. There are two other scenarios that could cause major concern and a downward spiral. One is stagflation which means no growth and higher borrowing costs. The other big imponderable equation is terrorism. Both can have a very negative knock on effect in the confidence of the consumer. But there will always be winners and losers which come out of every earthly experience.

Interest rate fluctuations are the main tool Alan Greenspan uses to keep the economy on an even keel. When interest rate fall, the economy should recover but overcapacity takes its time to work through the system. When supply exceeds demand profits plunge. We need to keep a close watch on signs of a recovery and act quickly, so we don't miss the boat. Once demand starts to outstrip supply, company profits surge and stock price reach new highs.

In today's markets the big money is earned in the few days in which the biggest movements are found. These movements happen in only about ten unpredictable days each year. The markets work six to nine months in advance of what is perceived to be the trend. We therefore need to see the light before it appears at the end of the tunnel. Spotting the bottom of a downward cycle is not easy but our gut feeling will give us a call once stock prices have reached a level whereby the seem to be in the last quarter of their decline. The genius inside us is constantly flowing with all the changes and we need very keen insights to pick up the messages. A little patience is a virtue but the main thing is to choose the correct signals our little voice is communicating. We should continue to investigate the best opportunities in each sector of the market. It is a top priority and an ongoing search for reliable information is essential for our ultimate objectives.

One of the most damaging ways of losing money is procrastination. There is no perfect time to invest. It will always contain risk ,but when we invest in a stock that has good fundamentals and is out of favor with the 'experts' we have a reasonable chance of a gain. The big question is how expensive is high. How undervalued is low. That is where the timing comes in. The more we investigate what makes the markets tick, the clearer our objectives become.

Having big expectations leads to big disappointments. When we expect certain results, we rarely get what we expected. We should always plan for all eventualities. If we keep an open mind and not pre-judge outcomes and events we will be ahead of most people. The stock market seldom acts how we expect it to. The randomness makes investing tricky for most folks. I believe it makes it much more fun. Where would the fun be if everyone guessed right every time? As long as we guess correctly, more times than we are wrong, we will earn money. There is no such thing as perfection so never expect anything, then we will always be happy with the outcome.

A perfectionist can be described as a flawless procrastinator and will not achieve anything in life for fear of failure. We are all going to make deficient decisions numerous times. Having more successes than failures will balance the scales in our favor. As long as we continue to gain a profit at the end of each financial year we are on the correct path. If we have a continuing downward cycle we need to change direction. Always remember none of us actually owns anything. Items we consider possessions are not permanently ours, the whole kit and caboodle is loaned to us We have the use of various items as long as we have a physical presence on earth. When we depart, they part our company.

The first lesson to learn is, everything is constantly changing and we must change with events. No perfection, no expectations, no blaming others for our mistakes.
We are now ready to progress through life on the wings of a dove and will soar like an eagle from one season to another. In a harsh winter we may need to stay grounded and just enjoy each day as is comes our way.

There are two meaningful effects to discern in life: firstly we want to attain our visions of wealth. Subsequently, we have to fathom how to treasure the joys of life, in its authentic form. Solely the true sage, accomplishes the second. M. L.

Sailing The Seven Seas Of Life.

When we arrive into this world, we enter as a ship that is navigated by the forces of nature and propelled by the power in the invisible auras of Spirit. It takes a few years for us to launch our ship with a self_propelled, man_made motor.

During this process we are taken to many shipyards for a refit to our intellects knowingness. We are trained by man_made ideologies and our natural awareness starts to go down deep inside the "Davy Jones locker" within us. We are taught to accept a new identity that will become the captain of our ship. We have to pass many tests of approval by our Admiralty of misguided intellects. Once we believe we are qualified to be our own pilot and navigator we set out to chart our voyage of a lifetime.

As we sail along on the seas of life's journey, we stop at many ports of call to pick up passengers and cargo. Some of these passengers become permanent guests in our lives. Some come for a short trip, as they were sent to us to fill a need. Our thoughts advertised we were in need of advice and guidance, so they came along for that part of our journey, for they knew the waters we were sailing. They steered us clear of dangers and helped us weather passing storms. Then they went on there way. Some died of a sickness or old age but their souls stay with us for guidance, as long as we know where they are located in our inner sanctuary. These were the angels that we asked to help steer our course. We still have our trusted physical crew all around our ship and we have to be aware that we need to treat them with love and respect or else we may encounter a mutiny.

We should always be on guard, for there are dangerous sharks and pirates in these waters. Many are after our cargo of money and treasures, whilst a few wish to take the joy out of our lives. The stock market is a vast ocean of scurvy forces that lie in wait to ambush us when we have lost our direction.

There are many other hazardous ships we will encounter on our travels and many fly the flag of friendship from a distance but when we get up close they hoist the skull and crossbones. Our lookout fell asleep and we were attacked because our vigilance was penetrated by impostors. Enemies posing as friendly sailing vessels in the seas of turbulent cross currents of information. And so we battle the storm and survive but each battle leaves its scars on our vessel.

Once we journey beyond our half way mark, we suddenly get the feeling we might be heading in the wrong direction. We start to understand the real enemy is within our own ship and the pilot we have so much faith in is an impostor. It is the same impostor that we have been battling in the other pirate ships, only this foe has been planted in our thoughts for many years and has grown in stature and strength. So much so it thinks it can control the ship in heavy raging seas, even when it knows the ship is aging and does not have the power it once had. When it realizes it does not have any real power, it wants to abandon the ship as it begins to sink. It wants to forsake the vessel and allow it to crash on the rocks of worry and anxiety.

The captain of our ship is a wimp. A false_hearted scalawag with no care for anything except its own importance. It is a stowaway that dresses up in a captains uniform recognized by societies elite and panders to their whims. That is why we believed it to be so real, for we have all been flying the wrong flags, because our captains are nothing but sophisticated, adulterated, decoys. The real captain is still onboard but held captive in the deep recesses of our vessel. Captain Ego needs to retire and become a quiet member of the crew.

The time has come to unlock the chains of imprisonment and allow our trusted captain to gain mastery of the controls of our ship. To escort us to safe waters where we can float on a tide of supreme bliss. Each day we will set out to achieve new goals and visit places beyond distant horizons. We will still encounter many storms along our cruises but with a steadfast captain at the helm, we will never fear any assault on our peace and tranquility. We have a twenty_four hour watch in the crows nest. Our finely tuned awareness is enjoying the true order of command. We have turned off the old worn out motor and we are sailing into the sunset with Spirits forces supervising our sail.

Within our life span everyone will sail the seven seas. We come into this world as a newborn baby and some of us leave within a day or two. We have still sailed the seven seas, only we did it in a pure vessel and in super fast time. Others may sail for over one hundred years. The time scale is not important. The quality and value of time spent joyfully is important. The seas are the same for everyone. Only the time frame is a little longer for some. In cosmic terms, there is little difference in a second or a hundred years.

The first taste is the banquet. The first sail is the experience of a lifetime. So we sail the seven seas of life until the time comes to set our ship adrift. We then sail into the infinite calm waves in the imponderable galax_seas of eternity. Until that day comes lets sail our charter on the authentic sensations of love & joy. Only Spirit can award us with a true captain and navigator. Each moment becomes a soul filled adventure of unsurpassable bliss.

Science is organized knowledge. Wisdom is organized life. - Immanuel Kant

No 2 Don't fall in Love with a stock!

This is one rule that should never be broken. It is essential to determine that *'It's a date not a marriage.'* If we start out with a positive accumulation of good habits, directions and spirit, we will reap many rewards. The questions we ask ourselves are:

- Why are we buying a particular stock?
- How long are we going to hold the stock?
- Why buy and hold for a long time?
- When are we going to sell it?
- What are our reasons for holding on?

Nearly every shrewd successful investor has always bought stocks when others are selling them in a panic and sold them when others are buying in a frenzied acquiring spree.

Barron Rothschild said 'I buy at the bottom and always sell too soon." These are true words of wisdom from a man who amassed a fortune. I don't know if he was 'a happy camper' but if he wasn't, then he could be miserable in comfort.

To Become a wise investor we have to buy stocks when they are cheap and they are the cheapest when everyone else is selling them. Look at the P/E ratio, look at the cash flow and if it looks cheap then it is worth investigating as a possible purchase. When we **"Buy low — Sell High"** we will make a profit. It can't be more simple than that, can it?

Just buying a stock, even a good one does not mean we are going to earn money on it. Knowing when to sell is even more important that knowing which stock to purchase. Owning a stock for ego sake is the dumbest reason of all for holding a stock. It is quite nice to say to folks "I own shares in Nokia or Intel" but how much better is it if we say "I sold Nokia at $60 a share?" At the time it might of seemed folly for the stock ran up to $80 a share, however, today as I write these words, the stock is trading at $ 19 a share.
Time to buy some? Well maybe?

Remember there is no such thing as a bad profit. If we allow the fear and greed factors to influence our decision making process we will buy stocks near their highs and when unpleasant news attacks we will panic. We will sell them when they are near or at their lows.

   So who do we listen to? Do we take advice from our brokers?
   If they know which way a stock will trade why are they still brokers?
   Why aren't they multimillionaires?

We will all hit a winning run from time to time and knowing

when to sell demands carful thought. Once we have bought a share we should set a target price and when that price is achieved we need to be disciplined enough to sell the stock. We will seldom sell at the top of its trading range. If it goes higher once we sell we should not get upset. Let's take this scenario.

Scenario A.

We buy 1000 shares at $25 after a few weeks it goes to $30 and we sell it. After a few more weeks it goes to $40. A few weeks later the stock hits $50. Now we are feeling bad. We call ourselves an idiot for selling to soon. We then listen to our friends brag how much money they are accumulating as the stock goes higher. They tell us what a fool we are selling so soon. We have 'only' earned $5000 on the stock but if we kept it we would now be sitting on a paper profit of $25,000. *But it is only a paper profit.*

Scenario. B

We buy 1000 at $25, it goes to $30 and we do not sell. The stock rises to $40 and we still do not sell. It now goes to $50 and we hear the analyst say the stock is going to $100. No way are we going to sell now. The companies results come out and they are bad. The stock plunges and within a few days it is trading at $15 a share. Now what feels worse? Taking a $5000 profit and missing a paper profit of $25,000. Or actually losing $10,000 of our hard earned money plus all the paper profit.

You see, we only ***GET A PROFIT WHEN WE SELL.*** Paper profits do not mean a thing. It is just mythical profits. They can and do disappear overnight. Remember there is no such thing as a bad profit. So don't ever feel bad if you make the wrong decision. There is no such thing as selling too soon if we have made a profit. ***"Paper profits are like unrealized dreams. If we do not live them, they never really existed."***

"It's Better in your pocket than theirs." Whoever they may be? There are 6000 stocks, therefore there is no shortage of selections. There will always be buyers and sellers. Bids and asks, shorts and longs, all competing to earn a few dollars the ***"easy way."*** It's a game played with others who require your money, so don't let them have it. There will always be winner and losers. Every day presents a fresh opportunity to continue the quest towards our goals. A $10 profit at the end of the day is substantially preferable to a $1000 loss at the end of the week.

If we trade stocks every day we will not be able to see the woods for the trees. When we have netted a profit or loss take it and go have a break. If it is a loss, wait until the next time we sense a good move. Never, ever, chase after a loss. Sometimes we need to wipe our mouth and get out of a losing stock quickly. We shouldn't carry over a loss to the next day if the news is detrimental, get out right away.

There will be many more opportunities. Wait for the next opening that has the percentages in our favor. When we trade from strength, we succeed, but when we chase after weakness we will fail. Learn to wait the moments of favorable percentages. Get the percentages on our side and never try to beat the ongoing trend.

There are many tales of woe the hi tech bubble debacle. Indeed there are enough tales of misplacing money to fill ten books. One chap had made a million dollars on two stocks. JDSU and Nortel Networks. He was wise enough to buy low and sell them at a great profit. As the stocks continued to climb after he sold he could not bear to see his beloved stocks climbing and not earn money. So he went back in and bought them back right at the top. The stocks were around $170 per share now trading at $8 a share. He is now losing a lot of his own money as well as losing all that profit. If that was not bad enough, there is a tax liability on the first sale of the stocks. Just one tale of very many.

I am sure as you read these words, you know of many folks who fell into similar traps. We will all make errors of judgment. What we must never do is relive the mistakes all the time. There is absolutely no point in beating ourselves up over errors caused by our greed. Many people fall into the same hole time and time again. History has taught us that it has happened continually since records began. Now our awareness is illuminating us to the fact we will not let it happen anymore.

Growth stocks fall the quickest and the deepest when growth rotates into stagnation. Value stocks have a cushion of having a low P/E and thus generally do not fall as steeply as stocks that hold high expectation. If we read this book once every few months throughout our life our vigilance in the devious nature of the markets will be paramount in our minds. We will refrain from playing the game with those who wish us to fall for the three card trick. In life we make our own luck and the wiser we become, the luckier we will get.

There are many theories and buy and sell techniques *"experts"* use. They have some value but as we are learning *"nothing is written in stone"* Some value fund managers use a disciplined approach when buying stocks. They only buy a stock when the market price declines ten percent from the same date one year ago. They sell a stock whenever the market is thirty percent higher than it was a year ago. They make a sell target and when the stock hits their objective they sell.

Most Fund managers are very disciplined in their approach and they try not to let their emotions gain the upper hand. If the value of the stock exceeds eight percent of their total portfolio, that usually becomes a signal to sell. Balance is the key to their safety net.

There are always exceptions to each rule and if they hold a star performer they may sometimes enjoy the show a little longer. But if they do not sell before the final act, the safety curtain will come down on the actors and many folks will get hurt.

Some investors use the "Dogs of the Dow theory" This involves buying the five lowest valued Dow Jones stocks. We have to beware of the dangers involved in this practice of buying stocks. Every now and then the lowest five stocks are replaced with new high flyers with a larger market value. Once a stock leaves the Dow, it must be sold by index funds so it could drop even more. That could be a great time to buy a quality stock. Many times it could possibly be oversold and will likely have a bounce once all the selling dissipates.

We can also short (sell) stocks as well as buying them. Risky? Yes very risky and I do not recommend shorting stocks, unless we are experienced traders with nerves of steel. Even they go rusty eventually. We are learning to invest without anxiety, so shorting stocks is a NO- NO.
The potential to earn money is limited on a stock on the way down, for it can only go to zero but it has no limits on the way up. If we still desire to short, then stock options may be the answer and we will be discussing them a little later.

Limit orders- are a good method of buying a stock at a price we consider fair value. If we have researched a stock very well and find a price we will feel comfortable with, we can place a limit order in the market.

Let's say we like a high tech stock called Wizzo. We want to buy five hundred shares. We do not buy them all at once. The stock price is $24 a share but we realize hi tech sales are weakening and could get worse. But the basic fundamentals of Wizzo are great and the future pipeline of produces will be market leaders.

Well, we don't want to spend all day looking at stock prices, so we can put in a limit bid price, to buy one hundred shares at $15 a share GTC
(Good till Canceled) and wait for the market to come to us.

If the stock price is hit and we buy the stock at $15, we are $9 a share better off than if we paid $23. We now own one hundred shares and it has cost us $1500 not $2300. Now if the stock continues to drop, we need to buy some more. So we put another limit order in at $13 another at $10 another at $8 and another at $6. This is called dollar cost averaging and if all the limit order prices are hit, our net cost will be around $10 a share. Now we can put in some sell orders.

If we have bought one hundred shares, each time we made a purchase, we can put in a limit order to sell one hundred at $10 another at $13 another at $15. We have earned $1400 and we still own two hundred shares trading at $15 a share.

Our investment has now only cost us $1400 for two hundred shares or $7 a share. The two hundred shares are worth $3000. We can now sit back and wait for the stock to double and treble in the coming years. Not much risk now and NO anxiety.

The fourteen hundred dollars is back in the bank or a bond earning interest, whist we wait for another good buying opportunity. The other two hundred shares are still making us more money.

When the stock goes to $30 a share maybe we can sell another hundred shares and put another $3000 dollars in the bank. I use one hundred dollar for ease of explaining. We could start with 1000 shares and dollar cost average down from the original purchase price in units of 1000 shares. When we start to sell the shares we have bought, we could sell in units of 900 not in the 1000 that we bought. That way we will build up a portfolio and it will not have cost us anything.

Now what if the price goes up right after we have made our first purchase. So much the better. We can take our profits sooner rather than later. We may not have invested all we wanted to but so what, a profit is a profit. We will rarely buy a stock on it's lowest price, so there is a good chance of buying more at lower prices.

The main thing to bear in mind when employing this method of investing is, always keep an eye on a companies fundamentals and if they change, head for the exit door.

Dollar cost averaging is a great way of building up a strong portfolio. The younger we start the better it gets. This method of investing is one of the best but I cannot emphasize enough, the cleverness comes from picking the correct stocks in the first place.

Wisdom is within us all. We just need to know how to tune into the success channels. The more we enjoy what we are doing, the more clear our decision making becomes and the more success we will achieve. Joy brings prosperity in every way possible. Listen to the melody in the whispers of our inner voice.

Day only orders;
We can put in a limit order and make it a day only order. There may be some news coming out the next day and we want to purchase a stock. We can place a limit order and see if we can buy the stock at a cheaper price than it is trading at. If we do not get our order filled, the order is only a day order and will automatically be canceled. We can always buy the stock on the close of trading.

Stop losses;
We own a stock and it has gone up substantially. We need to protect our profits. We could sell the stock when our instinct told us it was time to sell. Sometimes we may be a little undecided. A good strategy is to place a stop loss order, good till cancelled.

If the stock is trading at $40, we could put a stop loss on at ten percent below the trading price. Many times if a stock drops ten percent, there is a good chance of it dropping further. We would put in a stop loss price of $37 and if the stock comes down to that level it will be automatically sold.

The big danger with a stop loss is the company may come out with news after the markets have closed. The next day the stock could be cut in half. We will get only $25 a share because it has gone through our stop loss. An awareness of uncertain risks, leads to precautionary actions.

The IPO (Initial Public offering) market was up two hundred percent in 1999 and Down thirty percent in 2000 from the offer price. In 2001 many IPO's are struggling for survival. Many dot coms will not be around in 2002. IPO's are good in bull markets so wait for the cows to come home before charging into new offerings.

Too many people listen to tips from 'a friend who knows someone in the company' or some other 'expert.' etc. Blowing money on useless tips is detonating future opportunities. The stock market is a volatile trading market, therefore rule number two "*Don't Fall In Love With A Stock*," is a golden rule. Remember there are six thousand different stocks to choose from and change is good. There is no such thing as a disagreeable profit. Better in your pocket than theirs.

Ancient story.

There once lived a wise teacher who had a very keen student. One day the student came to class very excited and enthusiastic.

"Master I have now set my goals and my eyes are firmly fixed on them. How long will it take me to achieve them?"

"Ten years" was the reply.

No, you do not understand. My mind is firmly fixed on my goals. I am determined. How long now?"

"Twenty years" was the reply.

"If we have both eyes on our goals, then we have no eye on our path."

Let us, then, be up and doing,
With a heart for any fate;
Still achieving, still pursuing,
Learn to labour and to wait.
Henry Wadsworth Longfellow

"A fool and his money are soon parted."
Thomas Tusser

No one can make you feel inferior without your consent.

Eleanor Roosevelt

" whatever is flexible and flowing will grow, whatever is rigid & blocked will wither and die" Tao.

"It is not in the stars to hold our destiny but in ourselves." William Shakespeare.

Golden Rule No 3 - Market Timing IS Everything.

Many 'experts' will tell us it is impossible to time the markets and we have to be invested at all times. The events of 2000 and 2001 have proved this advice is a myth. Timing when to buy stock is the most important decision we can make, once we find the company of choice.

Many factors come into play before we make our commitment to purchase shares. Every day new statistics are released by the government and Wall Street reacts to them. We must therefore learn what statistics are due out each week and take action accordingly.

It is obvious to everyone that the hi-tech and manufacturing sectors jumped into recession from October 2000. This was due to a massive over capacity and a wilting demand. Supply and demand are the basis requirement for any product or service. When supply exceeds demand stock prices fall. This situation cannot go on forever and when demand picks up company profits will recover.

Inflation falling and interest rates declining at the same time, will cause a positive effect on stock prices. Even though company results may seem quite negative, if the products or services would be in demand in a normal economy, then we could be buying at bargain basement prices. This is when great buying opportunities arise. Markets work six months in advance, therefore as soon as there is a light at the end of the tunnel, prices will begin to rise.

Knowing when to hold and when to fold is the key to making money. Rarely, if ever, will we sell a stock at the top or buy it at the bottom. If we can make ten or twenty percent profit each time we trade, then we are on the ladder of successful stock market investing. Procrastination never made any one rich and panic selling will induce big losses .

When we do our homework well enough, we might want to let our winners run a while longer than just a quick trade. Going for a home run is OK but they do not come along very often. The key to getting a home run on a stock is knowing the sentiment is positive and getting in before big mutual funds. They will drive the price up and everyone else will jump on the band wagon. That's the time to Jump off. Contrarian thinking often pays big rewards.

We need to make careful decisions, then go for our goal. Become a strategist not a statistic. At the same time we need to understand Wall St. graveyards are packed with folks who were right to soon. Running out of money is no fun.

Good time management is essential to get the most out of each day. Voltaire said; "The world embarrasses me, and I cannot think this watch exists and has no Watchmaker."
Acknowledging the "One" who watches over us, will make our awareness of time more effectual, fruitful and productive.
If we are investing or running a business, we need to delegate and use our time wisely. We engage our time to instruct our staff to recognize how to excel in our absence. We make partnerships in all areas of our business wherever possible.
We make lists of actions to do each day and do the most important one's first. We prioritize way's to manage our clocks fingers, so that no seconds are wasted.

We list our goals and make time horizon on how long we think it will take to achieve them.

We take keen notice of the amount we have saved and how much more is needed to achieve our objectives

We begin to use time to make the most money, in the most cost effective way. We work to an agenda that does not waste a second and enjoy every second at the same time.

This gives double value from each of our moments on earth. We consider all the options when there are urgent questions that need answers.

Once we make a decision it is essential to take ACTION.

"If there are ten birds sitting on a fence and nine decide to fly away how many are left?"

The answer is "Ten." Just deciding to take action does not cut the mustard. We have to actually take the action.

Just deciding to do something has no meaning unless we carry out the action of our thoughts. Procrastination is the mother of broken dreams. Many folks who strive for perfection will never achieve their goal, for the is no such entity as perfection. We just do the best we can in all our endeavors and enjoy each experience, no matter of the outcome.

Make each moment more magical than the previous moments. With this way of thinking we become a wizard of effortless money making. Keeping our mind on what we desire, will put the forces of our creative mind to work. We guide our thoughts and actions in a positive manner, so that we achieve our objectives

Be mindful of the fact money is merely a means to an end and not the end! The end result has to be our happiness, otherwise all we achieve will have little meaning.

There has never been a teacher that can provide more wisdom than Silence. M. L.

What the wise do in the beginning, fools do in the end. _ Warren Buffett

Everybody thinks of changing humanity and nobody thinks of changing himself. _ Leo Tolstoy

No Matter what Being, Item or Thing we isolate, when we go back to its origin, we find it connected to the Universe. M.L.

The Skies of Pleasurable Desire

There's a heavy silence this breeze-less early morn,
A contrast to the chaos, the day cities were born.
Not a breath of air, the stillness of each leaf,
The splendorous picturesque landscape, beauty beyond belief.

The solitude is perforated by a happy mockingbirds song,
A prelude to the chorus, that will surely join along,
And sure enough, the air becomes magically transfuse,

*Via the ambiance of a choir, with technicolor, coordinated
views.*

*And now the scene is attuned for the Sun to take it's cue,
Conducted by a timekeeper, united to earths milieu,
The horizon suddenly awakens in a blaze of sugared crimson
fire,
Flames of warmth radiate, across the skies of pleasurable
desire.*

*A butterfly is formed, it's wings begin to flutter,
Magic is in the air, Love and Joy embrace one another,
The world has come alive, souls rejoice in dimensions drifting
higher,
Spirit orchestrates a unity, beneath the skies of pleasurable
desire*

No 4 Follow "Lucky" people who run large Corporations.
We become a smart stock picker by following 'lucky' people.
The more we practice, the luckier we become. There are some
terrific 'lucky' people running top corporations today. They
became lucky by lots of practice, shaping their own luck, so it
pays to follow them.

If we go into a casino look for a table that is winning. Then
look for a lucky face. There is always someone who is having a
lucky run, so we place our bets with that lucky person - follow
a winning team.

When it comes to the biggest casino, the stock market we can
place our bets with the guys who have proven themselves to be
people with wonderful judgment. Folks like:
IBM's Lou Gerstner, G E's Jack Welch (Now retired) City
Bank's Sandy Wyle and Microsoft's Bill Gates etc.

Some folks are just born leaders. These guys are just an

example of many leaders of corporations who are clear on the goals they want to achieve.

Research the heads of the companies you are interested in and play the game like you did in school --Follow the leader

There are many stars running Corporations, seek them out. The more questions we ask the more beneficial information we receive.

Story time.

Once upon a time in a far off distant land there lived a very wise old man. He was a true sage for he realized that he had all the answers he needed to enable him to live in joy twenty-four hours a day, every day. Who could ask for more?

One day he was walking on a path besides a large pond. Walking towards him was a young man with a turned down mouth and a sullen expression on his face. As he approached the sage he stopped and stared at the wise mans smiling serene face.

"Why are you looking so miserable on such a beautiful sunny day" the old man enquired.

"It's OK for you to ask such questions but you do not have my worries and anxieties. You do not have to pay my bills and debt." Replied the young woeful man.

"Come with me and lets sit over there on a bench. " This they did and there was silence for a few moments.

"Take this $100 note" The sage kindly said. "Thank you so much." said the young man, as he attempted to put it in his pocket.

"No wait, do you want your money to multiply?"

"Oh yes please" he replied eagerly.

"OK tear the $100 bill into 100 little pieces."

Without question the young man ripped the $100 bill to little pieces.

"Now throw them in the air" the wise man instructed.

Now more enthusiastic than ever, the young man cast the pieces into the air, expecting some magic.

A big gust of wind blew all the pieces far away into the distance.

"Now what have you done" enquired the wise old man.
" I have followed your instructions" he replied.
"Why didn't you question your actions?"
"Well, I thought you knew better" The disheartened youngster replied.
"You do not even know me, yet you trusted me?" the wise man smiled.
"You have an honest face" was the response.

" Do not take people at face value. Always question, then verify. Every day presents new opportunities and most of the time we squander them out of ignorance. If we take responsibility for our behavior and think of the consequences before we take any action, our results will flow and become successful."

"But how do I know what is going to happen before it happens" enquired the puzzled youngster.

"By asking many questions" came the gentle response "If we are going to invest our money in the stock market we have to ask many questions on the way our stock will perform.

We have to comprehend many of the possible scenarios which could occur and what appropriate action we will need to take. We need to recognize fear & greed . We then need to combat our emotions and understand the consequences such emotions can have on our ability to progress."

"But how will I know which questions to ask? What are the correct questions?" the young man apprehensively asked.

"There are NO wrong questions, only unasked questions. It is better to seem like an idiot for a few minutes, than to try and bluff our way through life and actually live as an idiot. Learn to enjoy all the treasures of nature and you will find true wealth and contentment. Material gifts will easily follow. When we remove the need, we remove the greed. When we remove the pressure and stress involved in striving for success, we become successful" the wise old man said.

With that he stood up and walked away, without the young man realizing he had gone.

The young man put his hand in his back pocket and took out his wallet. He looked at the dollar bills folded inside and thought. 'Now how can I best make this money work for me.

He then sat back and observed the ducks on the pond.
"Fall seven times, stand up eight."
Japanese Proverb
"The real measure of your wealth is how much you'd be worth if you lost all your money." Anon.
No problem can withstand the assault of sustained thinking. Voltaire
Time spent in adversity will bring out the best, from the best and the worst, from the worst. M. L.

Each Precious Moment.
In the cool damp haze of a morning mist,
Light filters powder diamond covered meadows,
This unfamiliar spring day stretches and yawns.

Inside vermilion dreams and crimson reality mingle in lucid

complexions
Eyes slowly focus towards the open window of infinite
opportunities
The world outside awakens to the milieu of song birds
serenade.

Tranquil connection effectuate sacred blessings
Gentle breezes caress the cheek, a fresh horizon is born.
Legions of ideas await the golden enterprises of the day.

Each precious moment becomes a priceless treasured Gem.

No 5 The first loss is the best loss.

Whenever we make a mistake get out right away. Never be to proud to admit we have made an error of judgment. We can sometimes get our facts wrong. Maybe we have been sold a red herring.

Perhaps we've been misled by an article or what we heard on a TV program. Maybe a well meaning broker gave us a recommendation. Everyone picks a looser once in a while and we must not dwell on it. Sell it and move on to the next. We may lose a few battles but we will win the war.

We must always keep on asking questions every day of our lives. There are NO wrong questions, only unasked questions. The responsibility to invest our money wisely is each individuals and no one else's. If we do not take responsibility for our well being, no one else will.

 If we go to a doctor ask him for the cause of the illness, don't just settle for treating the symptom. If he/she does not know then explore the illness more until the correct answers are found.

Once we dig a little deeper into our minds we find reasons why we are not progressing:

Fatigue- Fear- Anxiety- Lack of responsibility- Boredom- Lack of priorities- Confusion- Forgetfulness- Outside events- Compulsive behavior patterns- Depending on others to do our work.

Any of these signs can have a dramatic effect on our health. These are a few of the reasons why we get never prosper and become negatively affected into an illness.

We should research the cause of every action and what the effects of events and emotions in our lives will turn into when they happen. If we think about the many different scenario's that might occur in our life, then we will not be surprise or disappointed when one of them actual happens. If we have no precise expectations of an outcome and prepare for all happenings, we cannot ever be disappointed or let down.

When it comes to our investments, we should not wait until we have racked up big losses and then probe for reasons why. We need to ask the questions before we take actions then we will gain better results. A necessary requirement for sound investing is to keep asking question until we are satisfied with clear precise answers and then make our decisions.

Prosperity is a excellent teacher misfortunes is a greater one. Thomas Edison was asked by a reporter about his ten thousand failures to make a light bulb Edison replied I never failed once— I just found 10,000 ways not to make a light bulb. Walt Disney was turned down 302 times in his quest to fund Disney World. Colonel Saunders was turned down 1009 times as he went from restaurant to restaurant throughout the USA. It cost F. W. Woolworth's boss $1,000,000 for ever word he used to turn down his ideas.

Everyone will face adversity and losses. Even a loss must be enjoyed. It will make the good deals so much sweeter.
The greatest teacher of all is golden silence. Meditation is essential to obtain clarity of mind. Fifteen minutes of silence morning and evening should become part of everyone's lifestyle.

Remember these words.
There is NO REALITY, ONLY PERCEPTIONS.
Reality is a good or bad perception of our imaginary finite world. True reality is constant, everlasting, forever, never ending. Every moment events are changing and we need to learn we have to change with events.

Every cell in our bodies changes so why stick with stale thoughts. If we keep on making the same mistakes, we need to change course and find new direction. It's easier to have the wind on our back than in our face at the same time we fly higher into a wind. Life has no downside once we accept our true identity. We need to learn to take charge of our life and not to give away financial freedom. The best company to keep is spirits company. It is extremely comforting and brings infinite riches beyond our wildest dreams.
"Real riches are the riches possessed inside."
B. C. Forbes
Any fool can criticize, condemn, and complain - and most fools do. Dale Carnegie

We should always be aware of the pitfalls in a world of hungry hounds. We never get upset when we lose money. It will happen for sure because nobody can pick winners all the time. Everyone will have a financial disaster in their lives if they invest in the stock market or in the business world.

I remember the days when I was back in Manchester UK. I was a young, up and coming businessman, talking one day with an old wise businessman. He told me "Enjoy all your bad deals more than the good one's. Get a masochistic kick out of every bad deal you do" He said "Always be aware there are people in this world that do not have your best interest at heart. Life is full of deceptions."

It took me a few years to learn that lesson but it was one of the best I have ever learnt. Now I enjoy every bad deal, and never blame others for my actions. There are no down sides to life unless we make it so. We will meet many folks who may try to do us harm. The world is full of trickery. There are many con men around. We always have to be on our guard against those with evil intent

THE EVIL BROTHERS.
Many years age there lived two evil brothers. They lied and cheated all their lives. They were truly despicable but they did go to church every Sunday and put a lot of money on the plate, when it was handed round. The old pastor knew of their evilness but said nothing, for they were the biggest contributes of money, which the church badly needed.

The day came when the old pastor retired and a new young dynamic pastor took his place. The new pastor learnt of the evil ways of the brothers but he kept the status quo, and did not reveal their evil ways.

Time went by and one of the evil brothers died. The remaining brother approached the pastor and told him he would like a wonderful eulogy spoken at his brothers funeral. He wanted the pastor to tell the whole congregation what a saint his brother was. If he would agree he would give the pastor a check for $100,000. The pastor thought for a few moments then took the check and agreed to give the sermon.

The pastor quickly ran to the bank and had a quick clearance made on the check. The day of the funeral he went on his pulpit and delivered his eulogy. The church was crowded and he did not hold back. He told the congregation what a lying, cheating, repugnant, vile, nasty, evil person the dead mans was. He concluded with "BUT NEXT TO HIS BROTHER HE WAS A SAINT.

We will meet many folks in our lives, some are a God send and come along for a reason. We sent out a message and our call was heeded. Some relationships are brief, others last a lifetime. Some folks come into our lives and then with no wrong doing on our behalf, they may fall out with us. Everything has a reason. Everything passes in time. We cannot live our lives by other folks expectations. We must take charge of our own destiny.

That is why we must make a game plan and abide by it.
What do we want out of our life? Where is our comfort zone? We need to work out how much money we will need each year to cover all our expenses. Then we work out how much we will need for all our pleasure spending.
We then can make a budget and we will keep it up to date. Once we are contented with the simple things in life, we can cut down on our needs and wants. What we will find is the less we crave and demand, the more we will acquire.

When I first started in business nothing was wasted. The wrappings and string that our purchases were packed, were all recycled. After twenty five years in the same business, I still recycled all the wrappings, paper and string. Waste not, want not is a great motto. Make things out of nothing. In business focus on what makes money and forget all the fancy stuff.

Don't just accept the obvious. Look at other viewpoints. Never settle for "Normal" Make our home life and work fit together in Joyful pursuits. Create a synergy. No effort is involved when we are enjoying ourselves.

Just to be alive and experience every deal, good, bad or indifferent. It is quite sufficient just to enjoy the game of life. And it is, just a game. Whether it's the financial markets or the business world or just life in general. It Is **Just A Game** we play. Become a great player for life is far to important to be taken seriously.

"One fifth of the people are against everything all the time." Robert F. Kennedy

"Mediocrity knows nothing higher than itself, but talent instantly recognizes genius" Arthur Colan Doyle.

"There's no reason to be the richest man in the cemetery. You can't do any business from there." Colonel Sanders

To have hope, one must first be a believer-To be a believer, one must first have doubt-To have NO doubt of the truth, one has no need of hope or belief. M.L.

No 6 Don't get into Debt. The Piper Must Be Paid.
There are a few danger signals on the horizon that could lead to
a stock market slump for many years to come.
Some of the scenarios of doom and gloom are connected to
different types of debt in the financial markets.

Firstly there are fiscal debts the government builds up. The
USA owes the rest of the world six trillion dollars. One day the
piper must be paid. If confidence in the USA erodes it will spell
real financial trouble. When that happens watch out. It will not
be a pretty site to behold.

A large balance of payments deficit with the rest of the world
has persisted for the past twenty years. In that time span not
one month has been in surplus. This means the USA is
continually consuming more than it is exporting. More debt
than assets leads to a very dangerous scenario. If the rest of the
world loses faith in the USA economy, we could see Dow
Jones trading at 3000 or lower and bankrupts on a major scale.

When trust in the USA is absent, we will have a historic crash.
Since I do not possess a crystal ball, I do not know if or when
that will be. But we must look out for the warning signs. The
first sign will be a big rise in the price of Gold and other
commodities. A safe haven could then be Gold shares or gold
futures. It is not glittering at the moment. Is it time we had five
percent of our portfolio reflecting the glitter of gold? More

about commodities a little later.

With some three trillion dollars in the derivatives markets how do we know how healthy the financial institutions really are? It will not take to much to tip the scales and we may see a few bankrupt major institutions. Is it time we took a closer look at the finance house where our money is deposited?

Consumer debt is at an all time high. Savings are at an all time low nationwide. The consumers spending habits feeds stock market prices. The public must keep spending to sustain company profits. When they stop spending, the markets will fall. Down will fall baby, cradle and all.

Buying stocks on margin is only for the needy or the greedy. Going into debt to by stocks is a sure fired way to go broke. There could be a case for buying stocks on margin if you have other investments that yield a better return than the interest you are paying on margin. Even then it is a risky maneuver and it is a gamble.

There could be a case made to margin a stocks for a quick overnight trade if we have done all our homework on the stock. If we have large cash reserves then it may make sense to margin overnight if some news or results are out the next day. It is not always possible to send a check in time to the brokers to cover a trade, so a margin account could be of some use. Overall it is best to only put into the stock market, money you do not need to live on. Never put all your money into the stock market and never margin stocks with money you do not have. Never break these two golden rules.

You are what you think. Think like a millionaire you will become a millionaire. Think poor, be poor. $10,000 to a millionaire is pocket money, to a poor man it is a fortune. Nobody gets rich by paying high interest on credit card debt.

We get rich by accumulating appreciating assets. Save money and get interest, don't pay interest. If you can't afford something then wait for it.

Sometimes there seems to be a compelling reason why we should invest in a certain stock. If the stock has run up in price, don't go into debt to get in on a mania. This has been the downfall of many intellectual people who were swept away with the euphoria of the herd. Always keep a level head and chart a steady course, in the choppy waters of unpredictable markets.

We should not run before we can walk. Build up slowly but surely. Debt has become the normal way of living for many people. It may be "normal" but it is not natural. There is a big difference in living a normal life by societies standards and living naturally as the universe prescribes.
Many young people get into debt at University. Banks are only to willing to get bright students into the debt mentality. The smart ones get a part time job and either don't take out a loan or if they do, they pay it off in double quick time.

Anyone who is in debt should pay off any credit card debt first, before buying anything that is not essential. Pay the highest interest rates first. Stop pay 19.8% to the credit card Companies. If we take out $ 2000 worth of credit and we only make the minimum payments of $80(4%) going smaller as the principle is diminished. It will equal 116 months of payments and we will have paid $1215 in interest. Our goods are costing almost double and before we have finished paying for them they will probably be discarded. We should stop making the banks rich. Reverse the process and undertake a new determination in making ourselves rich. We need to earn twice as much when we buy on credit.

There was a character from a Charles Dickens novel who said.

One pound earned, spend nineteen shillings and six pence, result happiness. One pound earned spend One pound and sixpence result misery. A few things we can do to cut down on our spending habits are: Send letters with our own words instead of buying expensive greeting cards. Stop giving gifts until solvent. The people that love us will understand. Start to save a little each week as well as paying of any debt.

The Banks advice is in their favor not ours:-
A banker may tell us that we should use our home as equity to take out a loan, if we are thinking of starting our own business. They may even double our line of credit if we want.
Starting our own business has many risks attached. It is bad enough we are putting our hard earned cash into an enterprise that might fail and many new businesses do. Why should we risk our house in the process as well?

We should pay off our mortgage as soon as possible. Security is peace of mind. I know a lot of accountants will tell us that having a mortgage is cheap money but there is nothing like owning our own home, with no debt. We never put our home up, to buy stock or any other financial instruments, that we may contemplate. Even if we are opening a new business, we don't put our home up for security.

It is hard enough to run a business or hold stocks without the added pressure of a bank manager breathing down our neck, with his greedy eye on repossessing our home. If we want to sleep soundly at night, we will pay off our mortgage as soon as possible.

A Mans/Woman's home is their castle. We need to Guard our castle against those who want to take it away and we should rarely, if ever, take out a second mortgage to make more money. There are a lot of hungry hounds in this world. Don't become their prey.

Do you really need a big house, big heating bills, big taxes, big maintenance? Are the kids grown up and away from home? Is It time to find a smaller house with a nice big garden or a move to a condo?

What kind of insurance protection do we need. Make a list of possible cover i.e accidents. Divorce, medical, long term health, Life, Accident, Holiday. The fitter we keep our mind and body the less insurance we need from the outside world.

Mortgage insurance. Many times we take out a policy that goes to paying off our outstanding balance, should we die. Like all policies of this kind, it is incredibly expensive for the coverage we get. It is far better buying a term life policy big enough to cover our mortgage balance, if that is something we concerned about. The best policy is to keep our mind and body in good condition. If we never get sick we can save enough money and become our own insurance policy.

A bank is a place where they lend you an umbrella but ask for it back when it rains" Robert Frost.

We assume money and extravagance were the leading essentials of life, when all we need to make us joyous is the realization of just being alive is wealth enough. M. L.

No 7 The Greed Factor

One of the main reasons folks don't sell their stock is, they do not want to pay tax on their profit. This is the most ridiculous justification to hold stocks we can have. The worst thing that should happen is, we pay one million dollars in taxes EVERY YEAR.

This means we have gained at least two and a half million dollars each year. Always remember it is better to share our gains with others and even though we may not like the way the government sometimes squanders money, they also help a lot of folks in need. One of the most powerful propellers of the stock market is the Greed Factor:

Many times in our lives we read something or someone will act in a certain way and we will jump to a conclusion.
Most times it will be the wrong conclusion and we will miss out on our lifestyle in so many ways.
It could be in the investment arena. It could be our health or it could be our Joy.
Holding exceptions will lead us into anger and confusion, for we are programed to react from what we expect.
Wisdom has no expectations and enjoys each experience without any pre_judged conclusions.

A guy is having dinner with his wife in a restaurant. He say's "Daring when we were married you vowed you would love me for richer or poorer. Well I have lost all our money through my greed. Do you sill love me?" Of course, I do daring" she replied standing up "And I will write to you often."

THE GRAVY TRAIN

Take a ride on the Gravy Train,
clickerty clack on the track to a gain,
wealth and fortunes to a destination with no name,
no signals to stop, forgetting the station from whence we
came.

The journey of a lifetime, seeing love in money,
hands in the pots, grabbing all the honey,
no time to taste the sweetness, collecting all the jars,
blinded to the sidings, filled with rusty cars.

Looking out the window, see the years whizzing by,
still stoking up the furnace, driven to be the fastest to fly,
racing with all the locos, missing natures beautiful shows,
messengers with no message, answers only the devil knows.

Coming to the end of the track, alas no brakes,
Crashing into oblivion, ego is all it takes,
All the wealth piled high, smoldering in a heap,
Around in circles, in the abyss of the deep, mankind weeps.

If only love can be found, but where do we look,

Born in happiness, then consumed in misery, because fate overtook,

Bliss is waiting quiet and still, for us to switch on the power,

Time to use our own free will, arriving on Spirit's Hour.
M.L.

The greed element comes into many facets of our lives and it becomes a hard habit to break. A habit is something we hate but can't get enough of. Indeed all our emotions play a big part in our decision making. That is why it is imperative that we understand how our minds work and who it is inside our heads that is responsible for our decisions making.

Do we have any control over the decisions we make? We should ask ourselves "do we have the ability to make our own choices in life?" If the answer comes back "yes we do have the mastery to make our own choice" the next question is "why do we choose to worry?" Do we worry and hold anxieties, because we enjoy doing so?

I don't think we do like to worry, therefore something has gone awfully wrong with the way our minds work. If we cannot control our minds, then our decision making is flawed. If we are living by our emotions, it becomes impossible to make the correct evaluations when it comes to our investments.

There was a banker named Joe, who was a clever business man and he had two partners. Over a number of years they had built up a very nice small bank that was very profitable.

One day a takeover bid came to them and the Joe said he would like to take the offer and move on but the other two partners wanted to keep the bank and carry on. Luckily for them they listened to Joe, who wanted to sell, for they knew he had great foresight and judgment.

So they sold their bank at a good profit and went their separate ways. A few months later a big recession hit and financial stocks lost over half their value. The insight of Joe was from a higher level of intelligence. We all have access to this intelligence but many times our emotions get in the way and we can't see the woods for the trees.

Joe was not a greedy man and because he was satisfied with a comfortable lifestyle, he was able to take advantage of an opportunity that came along. In all our lives there are opportunities to excel but many times we are so preoccupied with our belief system, that we allow the opportunity slip by unnoticed. Every day presents us with an opening to make money in the stock market.

Just look at the movements of yesterdays market and you will find most of the stocks are either up or down. Lots of movements every day. Now all we need to do is preempt those movements in the correct way and we can make money. One of the secrets is not to be greedy. Never go beyond our capacity to take losses. Only put into the stock market money we do not need for everyday living. The older we are the less risks we take. If we never exceed our needs, there will be no need of greed.

∧∧∧∧∧∧∧∧∧∧∧∧∧∧∧∧∧∧∧∧∧∧∧∧∧∧∧∧∧∧

"Darling would you still love me if my grandmother did not leave me fifty million dollars." said the simple guy. "Darling I would love you, no matter who left you the money" came the flirtatious reply.

"I don't know much about being a millionaire, but I'll bet I'd be darling at it." Dorothy Parker

No 8 The Fear Factor.

What is it that gives us fear when it comes to our investments? The answer is simply, we are afraid of losing our money. A lack of security will give us fear. Each person has a different outlook on life. We all will react to a given situation in many different ways. For example, one person might be terrified of snakes, whereas someone else may walk around with a snake wrapped around their neck. A Person could be scared of heights. Another will sit on top of a high building with their legs dangling over the side.

To rid ourselves of fear, we have to rid ourselves of the attachment to the thoughts that gives us fear. To rid ourselves of thoughts, we need to understand what is real and what is an illusion.

Dispelling Phantom Fears

There lived a couple who had been married a long time. The wife was a very possessive lady. She became seriously ill. Just before she died , she said to him, "I've been attached to you so long, that I don't want to depart from you now. I don't want you to deceive me when I die. Promise that you will not see any other women once I depart. If you do I will come back to haunt you and never give you any peace." So he made his promise never to love another woman.

For several months after her death, he did shun other women. One day he met someone and they fell in love. On the night that they were engaged to be married, sure enough the ghost of his former wife emerged before him.

She condemned him for not observing the promise. Every night thereafter she reappeared to hound and plague him. She was aware of every thought in his head. She would curse and swear and would give him no peace. It perturbed him dreadfully and he found it impossible to get any sleep.

Despairingly he sought the counsel of a sage who lived near the village. "This is a awfully smart phantom" the wise one declared, upon heeding the man's woeful tale. "It is!" replied the man. "She recalls every element of what I convey and all my actions. She knows the entirety of every action within my existence.

The wizard smiled, "You should appreciate the fortitude of such a ghost. I will disclose what actions you need to take the next time your ghost appears.

That night the ghost returned. The man reacted precisely the way the master had advised. "You are such an astute ghost," the man said, "You know every thought in my mind.

If you can tell me the answer to one simple question, I will leave my fiancé and cancel our engagement.

I will become a monk and never see another woman "

Then without any thoughts in his head, the man scooped up a handful of beads from a large bag on the floor. He called out "How many beads am I holding in my hand."

Instantaneously the ghost evaporated and never returned.

^^^^^^^^^^^^^^^^^^^^^

We can only hold a fear as long as our thoughts dwell on the fear. Everything we see around us is constantly changing. We are changing all the time. Every cell in our bodies will be replaced over a period of time.

The only thing that does not change for many folks is old, stale, worn out thoughts of past events. We need to release our attachments to events and situations we have no control over. Once we learn to control our vision of reality, we can progress to live a prosperous life.

When it boils down to stock market investments, it is essential to learn to switch off the emotions. We need to gauge what our risk tolerance is and NEVER exceed it. Once we allow the greed factor to influence how we play the markets, fear will defiantly follow.

We will be helpless to cope with adversities. We will make may bad decisions based out of fear. To banish our ghost, we have to outsmart it. We have to go beyond what we know and follow a higher reality of intelligence.

That which fills the universe I regard as my body. That which directs the universe I see as my own true nature. Chang Tzu.

No matter how hard the intellect tries, to a foolish ego nothing is foolproof M. L.

Life begets life. Energy begets energy. It is by spending oneself that one becomes rich. - Sarah Bernhardt

He is a wise man who does not grieve for the things which he has not, but rejoices for those which he has. - Epictetus

No 9 Intuition (In -tuition)

How many times have we said to ourselves after a loss on the stock market or some other disastrous decision we made. "I knew I was doing the wrong thing. If only I would have listened to that little voice at the back of my mind." Just what is that little voice and where does it come from?

Intuition is the wise controller from which our instincts are continuously connected. The instructions and intelligence flow without any interference, justification or logic of the Ego. It is a voluntary, soundless, stimulation, from within, which is wholly liberate from any infliction of preprogrammed thoughts or ideas. It is purely free of the intellect and will feed the intellect when called upon.

Intuition goes beyond boundaries and once we learn to direct our focus on this indisputable power we obtain great insights into distributions of prosperousness. The word Intuition means we are in tuition. We all possess an educator enmeshed within us. Its wisdom can teach us all we need to comprehend for a successful life. Everything that has been discovered or will be discovered has always been here. We just need to open our awareness and tune into the correct wave bands and we can access the wisdom of the universe.

Intuition is our key to access wisdom. Most of our best decisions were originated from an instinct, born out of the genius within. Our flair and aptitude comes from an insight into our intelligence and that has been around well before humankind set foot on mother earth.

Our talents come to us from universal intelligence and if we are not aware of this power, we will not succeed in our lives. We will blame other folks for our mistakes and live with uncertainty and confusion. We will never attain our full potential.

Once we get a grasp that we are all part of a higher power, that we can see, touch, hear, feel or smell in a non physical manner, we become qualified to achieve great accomplishments. Life becomes magical.

We can learn a great deal from books but it took a genius to write the first books of wisdom in the first place. So do we desire to always be the reader or the genius who finds new avenues to explore?

The more the awareness of our conscious mind is sparked by our intuitions, insights, instincts, intuitiveness, inspiration, the more we progress. You will notice all the words begin with the letters IN. The word inspiration means IN SPIRIT. When we are illuminated with the forces of spirit, we become the genie of the lamp and we can grant ourselves the three wishes of Health -Wealth-Happiness. We can become an archaeologist and dig deep within our minds of inner space, to find the wisdom of outer space.

Investing in the stock market takes on new meaning once we become detached from the finite and attach to the infinite. We start to understand the way fear and greed move prices and we can act accordingly. In this way, we buy when stocks are cheap and most people are selling and we will sell when most folks are buying. We will also know there are periods when we will be sitting on losses but we know to wait and stay the course. Once we lose the ego (Ease Gains Out) the sooner we gain insights into wisdom

Intuition will beat any programmed information. We will become spectacular at reading between the lines of analysts comments and company reports. The president of Sony Inc. once said that if he has a difficult decision to make, he chews over, the deal and if it gives him indigestion, he spits it out!

Becoming a master of the emotions takes time and patience. If you don't know who you are or why you exist, the markets is an expensive way to find out the meaning of life. Anger is one letter short of danger and we will endanger our portfolio when we act with anger.

Fear rings the alarm bell of panic, then loses the holder in a maze of trepidation. Intuition is a power that lights up danger signs, then enlightens the path to safety. M. L.

Gratitude for Life on Earth

Within infinite light strings of kindled souls,
Galaxies of joy fill many mystical black holes
Quasar senses spark authentic mortal realities
Earthly pleasures set sail on mighty cosmic seas,

Magnetic waves flood humanities.

Within infinite light strings of kindled souls,
Merrily we consume loves delights from divine enchanted

bowls
Softly we taste enjoyment, whilst we hear silent gladness hum
We Rejoice as our tranquility dance's in a Quantum
aquarium

To the beat of the mystics drum.

Within infinite light strings of kindled souls,
Universal bodies shoot stars to score festive eternal goals,
Perpetual motions stir awareness with galas of appreciation
Gratitude for life on earth by spirits limitless celebration.
Time to Enlighten the Imagination of Every Generation.

EARLY HOURS

In my solitude in the early hours
I scale spectacular mountains,
I ascend high noble towers
I reside in peace-a house of no pains.

In my solitude in the early hours,
For desire I never hunger,
Neither worry nor hate devours,
I feel detached from my torment monger.

In my solitude in the early hours,
velvet darkness embraces me,
I sense the existence of universal powers,
As I savor divine bliss-empty emotions are set free.

In my solitude in the early hours,
Loves devotion consumes my woes,
Joy descends in illuminating showers,
As I begin to learn a little of what my Spirit knows.

Better keep yourself clean and bright; you are the window

through which you must see the world." George Bernard Shaw

Be a lamp to yourself. Be your own confidence. Hold to the truth within yourself, as to the only truth. Buddha

Be aware of the "Friend" that gives good advice. Their Trojan Horse may be filled with dangerous negativity. M. L.

No 10 Meanings of stock market value terminology.

Price Earnings Value— The P.E. ratio of a company is the most popular way to value a companies stock price. It is simply the price of the share, divided by earnings per share. i.e. If a stock is priced at $20 and the earnings are $2 a share the P.E. will be Ten. If other stocks in the same sector have a P.E. of fifteen then the company needs to be explored as a possible purchase. There may be a profit warning for future profits, so the P.E. could go up. Caution is required until the company is researched a little more extensively.

Book Value —When all the assets are added and all the debts, liabilities and liquidation price of any preferred stock is deducted, we arrive at a sum total of valuation. Then we divide the number of common shares outstanding to achieve a book value. This valuation probably will not match the share price. It is a good tool in understanding the true worth of a company if it had to liquidate. Sometimes the book value is lower than the stock price and could present a good buying opportunity

Cash flow valuation –The income a company reports. This valuation is important in determining if a companies stock is worth buying. If the cash flow is at a twenty percent discount to it's peers, then it becomes good value. The cash flow valuation also includes sums charged for depletions, depreciation, amortization and extraordinary charges. These charges are only bookkeeping figures and are not paid out in dollars

Dividend or yield Value— There are quite a few stocks that pay a good dividend. This is a good strategy for folks who want a steady income. Preference shares provide a good source of dividend income. Many banks issue good dividends on their preference stocks. These are interest sensitive and whilst the dividend is quite secure, the price of the stock will fluctuate with interest movements.

Riets; Real Estate Investment Trust, also yield a good payout. These are stocks that return income from property rentals like, shopping mall rents or perhaps hospital building rents. These securities also respond to interest rates, so a sharp eye on the economy is called for. The best time to buy these stocks is when interest rates are high and the best time to sell is when interest rates are low. Easy isn't It? Most folks do the opposite and although they get a good dividend, they lose capital on the stock price.

Takeover value— Many times a stock will run up on takeover speculation. Many times a stock will go down when the rumor of a takeover has been repudiated. If we trade on rumors, then the only way to earn money is to buy before the rumor comes out and sell quickly. If we can't buy before the rumor, then I suggest we don't buy after the rumor, unless we have more substantial evidence the takeover will go through. To buy on rumor alone is gambling and we can't afford to gamble, Can we?

Information value– There is a mass of information every day hitting us from all angles. What do we believe and how valuable is the information? We have CNBC. Continuously broadcasting data, from company results, to the price of cotton and orange juice. All information has a value and if we can sift though it, we may find a few gold nuggets. Many fund managers come on TV with a list of stocks they hold. Many brokers answer questions on Buy Sell or Hold. Also a CEO of a corporation may have some good news to announce. A few directors actual have good information and a stock can move a few dollars after their news has been aired. If the stock was up before they spoke, then it is not a good idea to jump in. However if the stock they are tipping has not moved and you can get an order to the floor in double quick time, you may be able to get a quick profit from a day trade.

Drip value investing ------ DRIP stands for dividend re---investment Plan. It simple means we can receive shares as an alternative to getting money from dividends. There is no fees attached to receiving the new shares and over a period of time the shares are compounded in value as the share price increases. This is a good means of building up a strong holding in your favorite companies. A company that gives a steady dividends which increase each year, along with the occasional stock splits, can make DRIP investing very profitable over a twenty year period. It is a sound way to grow a portfolio.

Equity valuation -Price of Stock is just the quoted price of the stock. It does not represent any indication to the value of the company and just because a well know stock trades at a very low equity price does not mean it is good value. It is not a good idea to buy a stock because the price "looks a cheapo" use the other valuations we are listing here. Being a Value investor has always been a good bet,

Perks valuation.– Many companies give discounts coupons to shareholders in their companies. Ask your broker if any of the stocks you are holding gives discounts for their products or services.

Convertible bond Values. A convertible bond can be exchanged for common stock at a given future date if the stock price hits a certain predetermined price. The bond will pay interest whist we hold it and we have the possibility of a capital gain if the stock price advances.

 Understanding values enable people to know in their own manner, what to do and what not to do. When valuations are clear, they do not have to rely upon directives from some "expert" adviser. By knowing what details are the most important, people can act separately from the herd.

In order to be a good writer or investor a person must have a good shockproof built- in crap detector. Ernest Hemingway.

 "I'd like to live as a poor man with lots of money." Pablo Picasso

"If you can count your money, you don't have a billion dollars." J. Paul Getty

The trouble with being poor is that it takes up all your time." Willem de Kooning

No 11 Mutual Funds

There are about nine thousand mutual funds and they do serve a purpose for the person who does not or will not give the time, to do their own investing. Do you know the name of your fund manager? Have you had a meeting with him/her? Who is looking after your money?

The average mutual fund charges four percent per annum to mange a persons holdings in the fund. This is quite expensive way of allowing someone free rein over your financial freedom. A stock management company could be a better alternative and usually charges a lower management fee.

Personally I do not subscribe to a club that wants my money and then charges me for it's use. The question we must ask ourselves is, who has the best vested interest in our financial well being? The one who is the most concerned , should be the one who handles our money.

The questions we should ask a fund manager before we hand over any money are:

How has the manager performed in comparison with the Standard and Poor's index?
Has the manager beat the S & P Constantly?
How long has the manager been with the fund ?

It the fund high risk or value orientated?
Are they accessible for questions every day?
Do they invest in stocks that don't come into their normal style
of investing i.e. Derivatives?

We should be aware that if we own a stock mutual fund we DO
NOT own any stocks. We only own the fund and in the past
two years four hundred and fifty funds have gone out of
business. The same is true of a bond fund. We do not own any
bonds only the fund that buys the bonds.

If we buy stocks in our own name and they go down in value,
there is always the chance the stock could recover and in time
we could still make a profit. If a mutual fund goes down it may
become to expensive to run and will close down. Many times a
fund will amalgamate with another fund run by the same team.
In this way they bury their mistakes.

There is another point we must be aware. There could be
adverse tax complications when we purchase a fund. At years
end we may face a tax liability, even though our fund has lost
money. Before buying any fund, check with the fund managers
about any tax payments that could develop in that financial
year.

Very few funds beat the Standard and Poor's indices over a
period of time. The good news is there is a way we can
become our own fund manager with no overhead charges other
than the brokerage fee.

There are financial instruments that cover a basket of stocks
and trade on the American stock exchange. They can be can be
bought and sold just like stocks and are very liquid. A few of
the indices that can traded are:

QQQ Nasdaq, This basket of stocks represents the top one

hundred stocks in the Nasdq

SPDR This indices contains the five hundred top stocks of the
S & P.

DIA this symbol includes the Dow Jones thirty stocks which
makes up the
top valued stocks on the New York Stock Exchange.
All three indices are traded on American Stock Exchange and
give the guy in the street a chance to be their own fund
manager. The indices can be bought and sold as many time as
needed in any given day. If we can find a trend, then this is a
great way to play the markets and not have to research
individual companies. It does require skill and knowledge of
world economies to be able to spot a change in trends and that
is where the genius within needs to be our informative guide.
The more volatile the circumstances, the greater the need for
clear and enduring fundamentals
No bird soars too high, if he soars with his own wings.
William Blake

We can live as a Miserable Prisoner or a Happy Guest in
our CELLS. M. L.

Every moment of every year is filled with love and Joy. We
only need to be aware of it's Presents. Who could want
better Gifts? M. L.

What we do not understand, we do not possess. - Johann
Wolfgang von Goethe

No 12 Rotation of Sectors.
One of the quirks of the stock market is the way herd mentality will downgrade a whole sector of companies. Stocks are categorized into a sector. This pigeon holing of stocks gives wonderful opportunities to buy a company that is doing good business but because a few companies in the sector are doing badly, the whole sector is downgraded. The "experts" have thrown the baby out with the bath water.

Diversification is one of the keys to successful investment management.
A few of the sectors are:
Growth stocks examples: Hi Tech, telecom's, biotech
Defensive stocks examples: Food, drugs. A safe haven in times of extreme volatility
Cyclical stocks examples: paper, engineering, these tend to do well when interest rates are cut,

Once a sector become out of favor, it could take quite a while for them to be recommenced as a good investment. Spotting the 'flavor of the month' is a useful method in finding the clues to making money. It is also a good guide in valuing other out of favor sectors.

Most fund managers act with a 'follow the leader' mentality and will sell unfavorable sectors to be able to buy into favorable sectors. This is one of the reasons why stocks become overvalued and undervalued. When asked why he bought an overvalued stock, one fund manger could only sheepishly say-

Bah!! Cause!!

A wonderful indication of a bear market is a big spike in the price of oil stocks. When oil prices start to increase it could be a sign of inflation and that is enemy number one for all stocks.

When interest sensitive stocks such as utilities start to move up, it could signal the start of a recession as interest rates are moving down to stimulate a sluggish economy.

If we can research the best companies within the out of favor sectors, we could produce a fined tuned portfolio that will reap rich rewards, once the sector become the darlings once again. Not putting all our eggs in one basket, will protect from having scrambled eggs for dinner every night. Whilst we wait, we just enjoy our ride on the merry-stock- go- round.

There is no Long Term anything. Nothing last forever in the finite.
Another big myth in the stock market is the notion of being a long term investor. No one lives forever, therefore there is no such thing as long term. There are some folks who buy a company and rarely sell. That is fine for them and if the correct stocks are picked a fortune can be amassed. That is how Warren Buffet made his fortune. However we are all not Warren Buffet and if we had kept many of the original stock of the Dow Jones, we would own bits of paper that are worthless. Buggy whip companies no longer exist.
"The secret to success is to know something nobody else knows." Aristotle Onassis

In this fast pace high tech world, only the fittest and smartest companies will survive. Even then, only a few of the survivors will hit it big. Out of the thousands of companies around today, only a few hundred will be really worthwhile investments over a five to ten year period.

Some may have a good run for a few years. That is why we must always set a sell target and when the stock hits it's numbers, we sell most of the stock. We can always keep a little holding in the company and if it is a real winner we will still get a good return.

Buying and holding any stock, even a potentially secure company, needs careful consideration. Keep the stock as long as the fundamentals are in place but also keep a sharp eye on global economy. If a recession comes along, even the good stocks could lose fifty percent of their value.
"Money is like manure. You have to spread it around or it smells." J. Paul Getty

It makes no sense to be a sitting duck and watch all our profits dwindle away, whilst the analyst is telling us to hold on and all will be well. We can always buy back a stock we have sold and most times it will be at a cheaper price. As they say in the casino 'there's a time to hold and a time to fold'

He who knows much about others may be learned, but he who understands himself is more intelligent. He who controls others may be powerful, but he who has mastered himself is mightier still _Lao_Tsu. Tao

We all dance to the tune of the mystical piper.
Albert Eienstein.

No 13 Be aware of Global News and possible outcomes.
In this world we can instantly access news twenty-four hours a day. The only tool we need is an up to date commuter . We can read a wide selection of overseas newspapers on line and find the opinions from different cultures.

There is a wealth of information in different countries newspapers. We can determine the likelihood of any global crisis a little sooner than most folks, who only read "their favorite Newspaper." If there is unrest in a small country it could have a major impact on the oil prices and it may not have been picked up by the mass media right away. Middle east conflicts, world peace, the gold prices, recessions in other countries and many other situations start from small pockets of discontent. Being alert to global news will put us ahead of the pack.

Another reason to read newspapers outside our domain is, how do we know how independent our news is from political censorship? Also how do we know what the owners of the newspaper interest are? Maybe they have big investments in other companies and they subdue any negative news from those companies. There are many other reasons why our local newspapers may not be impartial. An editor may be prejudice and have a narrow focus.

I know many such editors and my local newspaper will not publish poetry or any spiritual messages. The features editor told me spirituality is mumbo Jumbo and when I contacted the executive editor he told me that is the newspapers policy.

If newspapers take such a narrow view of life, then how can they publish a newspaper that tells the truth? When it comes to investments and business, are we are reading a reporters opinion rather than true facts? Do we get a true reasons why events are unfolding and effecting a companies share price? One days delay of the truth, can cost a fortune to big investors. We need the broadest and most concise coverage of information as possible. Keeping up to date in global affairs will aid our investment conclusions.

Change is a way of life. Everything is constantly changing and even if it is a change for the worst, we must be aware of it. Burying our head in the sand will only leave us with a mouth full of sand and emptier pockets.

There is a certain relief in change, even though it be from bad to worse; as I have found in traveling in a stagecoach, that it is often a comfort to shift one's position and be bruised in a new place. Washington Irving,

The winner of the Big race is the one who has finished last in many small races and continued to run a little faster each time. M. L.

Nothing ever built arose to touch the skies unless some man dreamed that it should, some man believed that it could, and some man willed that it must. - Charles F. Kettering

Only put off until tomorrow what you are willing to die having left undone. Pablo Picasso

Only in growth, reform, and change, paradoxically enough, is true security to be found. Anne Morrow Lindbergh

14 When Cash is king —Live Like a Millionaire.
Perceptions change the market in double quick time. Even if
we have spotted a trend, there can be many dramatic moves in
the opposite direction. Actions within any trend are all a
perception of each unfolding random event.

A golden rule is Never leave yourself short of liquidity. Always
have enough cash on hand to sustain your lifestyle whist your
stocks recover from a steep fall. A collapse in share prices can
happen overnight by global events or unexpected home
happenings.

Uncertainty is a big foe of upward trends, therefore it is
essential to have some cash in the bank to be able to take
advantage of one off openings. Be prepared to take advantage
of buying opportunities. When everyone else is panicking, you
can be picnicking.

Get interest on money instead of squandering it. Poor folks
spend borrowed money for depreciating assets i.e. cars,
electrical goods, designer cloths, etc, to impress others and pay
double. That is way they stay poor. Millionaire dress down and
don't squander their money.

One rule everyone must know if they want to accumulate
money is:
The Rule of 72. This rule indicates the number of years it takes
for your money to double i. e.
 72 divided by a return of 9%= 8 years.
72 divided by a return of 12% = 6 years.

If a 20 years old invests $10,000 at a rate of 12% and retires at the age of 65, they will participate in 45 years to growth. Their money will double every 6 years. Compounded 8 times it would be worth $2.5 million. Not a bad return and a very nice nest egg for the years ahead.

A true millionaire knows how to win and can accept success graciously. They Do not fight the odds but makes the odds. They may lose many battles but they stay the course and win the war.

To become a millionaire we need to live like a millionaire. We should buy when we see a bargain for any future events in our life. The government recently calculated the cost of raising a child from birth to 18 and came up with $160,140 for a middle income family.
Planning and buying ahead of events saves time & money. We don't buy clutter, we buy quality at a low price. Don't squander money on unnecessary clutter.

When you see an ornament or a handbag ask yourself do you really need it. If it brings real joy buy it, if not leave it. Look after the pennies and the dollars will look after themselves. Don't try to impress the neighbors, true friends really don't care about your possessions

They say women was born to shop and man was born to hunt and fix things. The shop till you drop psyche, deprives us of time from investing. Time grows money. A shopping mentality need a fix compensation for love and attention, from shop assistants pandering to our emotions. Many women are changing and are becoming great earners and investors. They know time can be money and fun.

The ego's of men enjoy big buys such as; cars, computers, hi fi's. They want the fastest, the latest, the best, with all the bells and whistles. They relish competing and bragging about their expensive toys. Many time they go into debt to buy depreciating assets. We will never get rich this way. Millionaires are more disciplined. They Buy Only what they really need.

Money behavior is not discussed until there is big debt. It is a big mystery to folks when the piper has to be paid. Thus money become one of the main reasons for divorce. Old habits are hard to die even in a modern world of equality.

Here are a few more habits we can adopt to live as a millionaire lives. When we learn to cut a few corners, the path ahead becomes straightforward and the journey is more comfortable.

- Learn to cut your own hair. Snip away and save the pay.

- Do it your self at home. Decorate paint the house, Renovate.

- Keep your main asset in tip top condition. You will get top dollar when you sell it. learn to fix broken pipes and repair electric circuits. There is more money left on the shelf when we do it our-self.

- I know millionaires that shop at thrift shops what's good for the goose is good for the gander..

- Get doggie bags from restaurants. It Makes a good meal the next day. Woof! Woof!

- Cut coupons and put the money you save in a money box, then bank it at months end. Look after the pennies and the dollars will look after themselves

- Turn the lights out when not needed. Stop making the electric company rich. Don't burn money, it does not make good firewood. Best to burn newspapers.

- Make your own birthday cakes and cookies. They will be healthier and cheaper. Feast and save.

- Grow your own veggies. Organic is healthier also.
- Cut down on meat dishes. Eat fish and chicken. Eat like a kings and queens.

- Use email not snail mail. Save and deliver.

- Pay credit card right away. It is expensive money to borrow.
- Neither a borrower or lender be.

- Do you really need all the cable TV? Reduce what you watch. Most is senseless rubbish. Become more productive with your time. Time is our most priceless asset spend it wisely.

- Do you really want to read all that negative news first thing in the morning? Cancel the newspaper. Reduce the negative aspects of your life. Be choosy and look at the internet for news you wish to read. It also stops the hands from getting black ink on them. Read a good book instead.

- Swap phone Companies regularly. They give money or free phone time. 'Ring' around of roses.

- Go to the discounted afternoon matinees and take an apple with – don't buy their expensive candies and Popcorn.

- Watch happy, funny movies. If we want to see blood and guts, we can look at the stock market!! Go to be entertained not depressed.

- Don't buy "dry clean only" Clothes. Wash and wear.

- Learn to sew. A stitch in time saves nine.

- Quit smoking, live longer and save money. Same with alcohol. Pack it in, you don't need it. It's false enjoyment.

- Drink water or fruit juice not soda. Dilute the fruit juice it goes twice as far and we consume less calories.

- Take sandwiches to work don't eat out. Go to a park and enjoy the birds and the bees. Smell the roses.

At the weekends play games with the kids instead of looking for expensive outing. Make your own amusements. It gets you closer to your family. Learn to play a musical instrument. Form your own group or quintet. You can start to charge for performances after a while. The possibilities are endless. Go back to the "Good old days" for the moments are precious and go so quickly.

Why take the car when you can walk? You will save money on gas and get healthier workout. Keep exercising and keep healthy. Prevention is the best cure and it will save money. When we keep ourselves healthy, we keep away from doctors.

Clear out the attic you might find a hidden treasure. You never know what you might find. Old toys fetch big bucks.
Hold a garage sale instead of just throwing stuff away. Be

professional in the layout of your stall. Buy or make interesting 'for sale' signs and put well made price tags on all merchandise you wish to dispose. Advertise all around the neighborhood with "big sale" notices.

When you have acquired a fair amount of savings treat yourself. Spend a little silly money from time to time. Treat yourself for being smart with the budget. Have a Massage and relax.

If we leap to far to fast we may need to backtrack a little. If the gap we made is too large we will jump into the hole we made. M. L.

Success grows on the Tree of Wisdom.
Do you think its time to visit the branch manager? M. L.

Our scientific power has outrun our spiritual power. We have guided missiles and misguided men.
Martin Luther King, Jr.

Life's Tragedy is that we get old to soon and wise too late.
Benjamin Franklin

We judge ourselves by what we feel capable of doing, while others judge us by what we have already done. Henry Wadsworth Longfellow

No 15 Go on the Internet to check out Hotels, Cruises, Holidays Car Buying ETC........

There is a wealth of knowledge on the internet. With over two billion pages we can find information on just about everything. The world is at your fingertips. Lots of freebies, Knowledge, Libraries etc.

A car is one of the major items we purchase so it take careful thoughts before we make a buy. If we are seriously contemplating purchasing a car, then the internet can really be a big help. Check the invoice price at -Edmunds.com and Option extras packages at cost. Look at - Cars Direct.com and Greenlight.com. Once we are armed with all the cost details we have the knowledge to make a great deal.

Dealers have a "Hold back" of 2-3% from the manufacture so buy your car at invoice price. Go the showroom at the end of the month. If their sales have not been on target they will be more likely to give a good deal. Don't mention a part exchange right away if you have one, or they might low ball your part Exchange car. Negotiate the cheapest deal you can get, then mention your car. See what they will offer you. Then try and sell it privately. Don't commit to buy right away unless you know you can't do better. If they will not come down to the price you want to pay, then walk away. They WILL phone you back a few days later and meet your price.

The car dealer will try and sell you a car with lots of extras. Ask yourself if you need all the bells and whistles? It's money down the drain. You will not get any more money when you come to sell the car. Don't get sucked into buying all the extras

unless they are 'thrown in!'
Get your own finance if you are not paying cash. Some dealer get an extra 2% from the auto loan company.

Most times it is better to buy then lease. In the past it was a good deal to lease but the banks have wised up after they lost money on overvaluing residue values of the car. A Lease also costs more because fewer people haggle on the price. There could be tax advantages to leasing if it is used as a company car.

If we think along the correct lines everything we do in life is good. Seeing the bright side of life in all situations make for smarter deals and a happier life.

Story.
A University professor was addressing the school and telling them about an old lamp the caretaker had found deep in the basements of the building. He held up the lamp and as he did the lamp brushed against his jacket. Out came a magic Genie. The Genie said you may have Money, Wisdom or Beauty. The school held their breath whilst the professor thought. I will take Wisdom the Professor Replied. There was an almighty flash _ then silence for two minutes. A little voice from the back of the room yelled "say something." "I should have took the money"declared the professor

When things aren't going as we planned, enjoy the experience and make new plans.
If there is light in the soul, There will be beauty in the person.
If there is beauty in the person, There will be harmony in the house.
If there is harmony in the house, There will be order in the nation.
If there is order in the nation There will be peace in the

world. (Chinese Proverb)

The internet is the best place for research before making any purchase. We should not buy on an impulse. One of the best avenues to launch a research for attractive stocks to purchase, is to observe which insiders are buying their own stock. Likewise we can view which insiders are selling their own stock. People can sell for many reasons but only buy because they think they will earn money on the purchase. If the people who work for a corporation are willing to put their money where their mouth is, then it is worth investigating further

Money flows into sectors, Check what's hot and what's not. Follow the trend patterns and don't fight the fed. They say the tapes never lie but they don't go in the direction we expect either. If we can spot the beginning of a trend we will make money

Many analysts follow chart patterns. They can give an indication of a trend and many times when we see a chart and it looks like two mountain peaks or a double head that often signals a downturn in the companies fortunes. It is worth while taking a look at a one week, one month, one year and three year chart of a company we are considering investing in before making a commitment.

Studying the balance sheet of a company we are interested in is just plain common sense but how many people do it?
A companies latest balance sheet is always available on request. There are also company 1- 800 numbers we can contact, to gain more information on how the company is performing.

Fundamentals:-
Daily statistics Every day produces a host of statistics from all over the world. Pick out the one's that move the markets the

most and check on them each month as they are released. many statistics will move the market in the opposite direction of the trend of a stock. Many day traders wait for days when important statistics are release and act on the information.

World news is important, so keep abreast of financial and political news in all the major countries that could effect our financial status.

Weather can have a dramatic effect on many stocks. Droughts or floods will move prices in food and insurance. stocks. Keeping an eye on the weather will help us save more money for a rainy day.

Understand the Stock Market Information.
Exchanges:

- **Nasdaq-** National Association of Securities Dealers Auto Quotes.
- **New York Stock Exchange** -Blue chips and better regulated.
- **American Exchange-** Options, index tracking stocks.

Many on-line quotes have a time delay of 20 minutes.

- **Always get** a real time quote before a share transaction.

- **Ask for the last price traded**.

- **Check out---** the percentage change on the stock from the previous close.

- **Check High----**Low for the Day

- **Check High—** Low for the year.

- **Check the Opening trade** ----- What price was the first trade of the day.

- **The Volume** is an Important indicator.

- **30 day Average Volume;** When you see a larger than average trades for a day or more, there is something going on that needs investigating.

- **Check the Beta number–** It indicates the stocks volatility.
  Less than 1 then the stock has gone up or down less than   the market. Over 1 the stock has gone up or down more   than the market. Aggressive investors like a big Number .Defensive look for a low Number.

- **Check the Yield:**   It gives the amount of dividend paid on a percentage basis.

- **Check the P/E Ratio Price** of the stock divided by earnings.

- **Check the EPS-** earnings per share. The last four quarters added together. The higher the better.

- **Settlement Date:** The date on which payment is made for a trade. For stocks traded on U.S. exchanges, settlement is currently 3 business days after the trade. For mutual funds, settlement usually occurs in the U.S. the day following the trade.

A Few Financial Web Site To Explore:

1.   Netstocks direct.com----

2. Buyandhold.com—
3. Gomez.com
4. Tulipsandbears.com
5. cnbc.com insiderscores.com ----
6. personalfund.com-----
7. Lionshare.com–
8. BulldogResearch.com
9. companysleuth.com—
10. valu-engine.com----
11. Marketocrcy.com--
12. FreeEDGAR.com
13. mystockoptions.com---
14. financenter.com-
15. directadvise.com--
16. worldlyinvestor.com--
17. onmoney.com
18. fundinteractive.com——
19. smartmoney.com
20. quicken.com----
21. fairmark.com
22. outercurvefinance.com--
23. wevest.com-
24. investor.com-----
25. prophetfinance.com—
26. Investavenue.com
27. On line brokers----
28. DLJ Direct.com --
29. Schwab.com –etrade.com
30. Fund Info.
31. Morningstar.com-----
32. fundalarm.com------
33. maxfunds.com----
34. idayoinvestor.com--
35. indexfunds.com-----
36. mfea.com(No-load funds)
37. sec.gov(SEC filings)

38.   validea.com--
39.   riskgrades.com

**Something we were withholding made us weak Until we
found it was ourselves. Robert frost.**

**When you were born, you cried and the world rejoiced; live
your life so that when you die, the world cries and you
rejoice. Cherokee Proverb**

**Everything comes to him who hustles while he waits.
Thomas A. Edison**

No 16 Listen attentively to Alan Greenspan. Don't ever
fight the Federal Reserve. They control the money supply. It
can be turned on and off like a tap and we do not want to
drowned in an overflow or die of thirst in an arid desert.

Mr Greenspan has a great financial instinct and has navigated
the USA economy on an even keel for many years. It is wise to
take heed of what he says. In fact it is also smart to heed what
he does not say. Reading between the lines can forewarn us of
upcoming moments in interest rates.

Interest rates dictate the direction of many stocks. They make a
wonderful barometer for tomorrow. Economic fundamentals
such as signs of Inflation and recession will cause the Fed to
take action. Since markets discount events six months in
advance, early warning detection signs are required.

Well before the high tech bubble burst, Mr Greenspan was
warning of 'exorbitant exuberance' The warning signs were
there. Most folks ignored him and persisted to blindly throw
money at stocks, that had no earnings and no prospect of ever
earning a profit. It was working well for a while and many
people thought why listen to that silly man.

Many people thought of themselves as an investment guru's
and were jovially tipping stocks to all and sundry. Even a
stopped clock is right two times a day! Anyone who tried to
warn them of upcoming troubles was called an idiot and
ignored.

Well that silly little man named Alan Greenspan turns out to
be right after all and those who listened saved themselves a lot
of grief and lost assets.

Although Alan has not express that the markets are acting with exuberant pessimism after losing much of their value, he has remarked how he believes High Tech stocks are the future motor to propel the USA economy. What goes up must come down and no doubt will rise again.

True philosophers who are burning with love for truth and learning never see themselves . . . as wise man, brim_ full of knowledge . . . For most of them would admit that even the very greatest number of things of which we know is only equal to the very smallest fraction of things of which we are ignorant. Nor are these philosophers so addicted to any kind of tradition or doctrine that they suffer themselves to become their slaves, and thus lose their liberty. William Harvey

An aim in life is the only fortune worth finding.   Robert Louis Stevenson

Negatives see life in Black and white
When we develop a positive focus we see life in color.
The Mind is a Dark room for development M. L.

The more we suffer, the more the Soul craves for recognition. M. L.

A person starts to live when he can live outside himself. Albert Einstein

No 17 Life is full of options. Stock options is one of them.

They say life is what happens whilst we make plans and option trading can help our life savings. One of the most effective ways we can protect our share holdings is by implementing options as a hedge against severe downward movements. There are two types of options:
Call Options reflect the purchase of a stock
Put Options reflect the sale of a stock.
These are the basis of traded option for the average person.

Call options gives a person the rights to purchase a stock at a specified price, on a certain set date in the future. When we take out the option, we do not actual own the stock. We are buying time to purchase the stock at a given price called the 'Strike or exercise price,' before or at the expiration date of the option.

The price we pay is called the premium and this price depends on the length of time the option has to run. Volatility is also a major factor in the price of the option. The value of the option has two legs.

One is called the intrinsic value, the other the time value. The intrinsic value is difference between the strike price and the actual price the stock is trading at. When we add the time value on to the intrinsic value, we arrive at the price we can buy or sell the option at that moment in time.

Once we purchase a stock option, we can sell it at any time before it expires. We also have the choice of actually taking delivery of the stock at the time of expiration. This is called exercising our option.

A put option gives us the right to sell a stock at a given strike price. This is the safes way to short (sell) a stock without ever buying it. It is also a good way to protect the stock you own without actually selling it. As with the call option, we can sell our put option any time before it expires

Here is an example of a Call option.

Stock A1 is trading at $22 a share on the open market. We would like to purchase one call option, which is one hundred shares of stock in A1. We phone our broker to get a quote on an option that expires in one months time. Today is the 22nd of Sept and the option expires on the 21st Oct.

All stock options expire on the third Friday of each month. We are quoted $3-50 for the option. The option has an intrinsic value of $2 because we are buying the right to purchase the stock at $20 on the 21st of Oct. The stock option is "in the money." We are being charged $3-50 for that right, so we are paying $1-50 extra for the time value of one month. This option will cost us $350 and we own the right to purchase 100 shares at $20.

This has saved us $22,00 outlay. Our money is in the bank earning interest and we "own" the stock for one month. The next week the stock is trading at $25 a share. We phone our broker and sell the option. We get back $5 which equates to $500. We have lost a little time value of 50 cents because one week has gone by. But we have earned $1-50 ($150) which is about a 40% profit in only one week. This is a great way to leverage our money when it works out well.

Now let's take the same amount $3-50 and keep the option until it expires. The price on expiration is only $22 so the option is only worth $2-00. We have lost all the time value and will get back $ 200. A loss of $150. If the stock is trading at $20 on expiration, we have lost everything and the option is valueless. The price of the brokerage fee has to be calculated on top of the price we pay for the option.

Dealing in put option is the same, only we require the share to go down in value and then we earn a profit.

Options are very risky financial instruments and Many times they become worthless. We need to time our tactics with expert precision to finish ahead of the game. The best periods to play the option market is in times of high volatility. When there are wild swings, a large amount of money can be made with little outlay. We are limited to the size of our losses by the amount of money we pay for each option but our gains are unlimited.

When there is little movement in the markets option price do not move and we lose the time value. Sluggish markets are NOT a good time to buy options, unless we own a stock with exciting, breaking news, that will move the stock. The genius within us can work wonders, once the wheels of the mind become well oiled with spirits magic formula.
Keeping alert to the opportunities that come our way will pay big rewards.

Story Time.

Once upon a time there was a young man who was broke. He was walking around town looking for work, when came upon a beauty parlor with a sign in the window. It read "Help Wanted"

He went inside to enquire if he could get a job. The owner said they required a clerk and asked the young man if he could read and write. He said he could neither read nor write, so the lady expressed her sorrow and said she could not employ him. As he was leaving she felt a little sadness, so she gave him two beautiful peaches to eat, for she could tell he was hungry.

The young man left with the peaches and was walking down the main street and put his peaches down on a table next to a newsstand , so he could read a newspaper. A passerby enquired the price of the peaches and as quick as a wink, he had sold them.

With the proceeds, he went down to the fruit market and bought more fruit, which he quickly sold. In a month he had a stall on the market. In six months, he opened his fist shop. In ten years, he owned the biggest supermarket chain in the state.

One day he was being interview by a reporter and he told her his story. "Wow that is fantastic" remarked the reporter. "But just think what you could have been if you could read and write" and the reply came back "Yes, I would have been a "CLERK IN A BEAUTY PARLOR!!"

What a wise man will teach in a few words, an Intellectual fool will not be able to express in a lifetime. M.L.

All mankind is divided into three classes: those who are immovable, those who are movable; and those who move. - Benjamin Franklin

No 18 The Commodity Markets.

Commodities are an intriguing way to make a little money from a LOT of Money, if we are not very, very, very, careful!! They are after your money. Who are they? I do not know who they are but they will take your money if you trade on a daily basis. Only one in a thousand earns money in these markets. THE " HOUSE" ALWAYS WINS. They are the croupiers. It is a thrill a minute until the money runs out.

The commodity futures GAME is a MONEY GAME. NOT a game involving the supply and demand of the commodity, as we rarely take delivery of the commodity.
It is a Money Game with bets on the future direction of their value.

Mass group perception is more important than fact, when it involves market movements. That is why logic rarely works. Markets work on a supply and demand basis, with a little manipulation thrown in for good measure.

We need to display the insights of a prophet, to be able to earn a profit. Predicting the future with or without a crystal ball is no easy task. We need nerves of steel to become a trader and I do not recommend round-the-clock trading unless you have developed a unique trading technique.

So if they are so impossible to predict ,why am I talking about them? They do have their usefulness. Keeping an eye on the way commodity prices fluctuate can give us a good handle on the direction the stock market may go.

The commodity market is highly leveraged and large contracts can be taken out for a small amount of margin money. A trade can cost just $20 but a margin account has to be set up and a reserve amount of money is needed to maintain the account. When the maintenance amount becomes depleted, a margin call is announced.

The golden rule here is 'Don't over leverage.' The biggest mistake a trader makes is buying a commodity with a small amount of money and not having enough in reserve to sustain the position. Liquidity in the market is a driving force. When there are many margin calls, the commodity will change direction when all the leveraged traders are forced out.

There are always hard luck stories. The 'if only's' and the 'just misses.' It is like the fisherman with his tale of the big fish that got away. The answers is; little fish are sweet. Little profits beat big losses every time. The more money we have to start with, the better the chances of success but it could also mean the more we can lose. We should practice many dummy trades, before we take any chances.

Risk-reward is always to be considered before we place our bets. If we take a commodity to go down, the risk is unlimited, for the sky is the limit when it is going up and there is no ceiling. If we take a commodity to go up, the risk is limited to the price going back to zero. We can only lose a limited amount. So the big risk is when we short a commodity.

I am not advocating that we should even be trading in

commodities but it helps to know how commodities trade, so that we can become a smarter investor with our stocks.

Chaos theory -Within all markets there lives a period where chaos becomes a hurricane force that disrupts a trend. It is a highly random movement within a trend component. Trends varies from time frame to time frame. It is impossible to predict future events when chaos appears but short term movement can be guessed a little more accurately.

If Greenspan is going to talk on interest rates, we can guess if he is going to soften or harden the rate. A few days before he speaks there will be a lot of hype from the business part of the media, that will scare folks into action. Then when it becomes apparent that it is not as bad as they predicted, the action will reverse. Many times it's up on rumor, down on fact.

In between this time frame, a catastrophic world event can take control of movements. The Result is chaos and market pandemonium. This movement often reverses itself back into its original trend. Because of this chaos theory, the markets can be a graveyard of hard earned money, that has taken a lifetime to save. Let the Trader BE-aware.

Some of the major commodities to keep a close watch over are: Currencies, Precious metals, Oil prices and interest rate futures.

The Dollar is the currency of choice for all commodities and every commodity is priced in dollars. Keeping a close eye on the value of the dollar as it trades against other currencies, can be a guide to investing in overseas markets. If we sense the dollar is about to weaken against other major currencies, it might be a good signal to buy stocks in those countries.

It could mean the economies of other counties are on the up and it is time to go shopping and buy some of their great corporations. If we live in the USA, we can get a profit when the stocks of a foreign country go up and also a gain on the currency exchange if the dollar has weakened, when we sell the stock.

If we want to buy a stock in a foreign country and the dollar is strengthening against other currencies, we can hedge our position by buying dollars one year forward, on the commodity market. That way we 'lock in' our dollar price and only have the stock price to follow. Our dollar price is protected for a year with our forward purchase of dollars, against the currency of the country we are investing in. This is one way of making good use of the commodity markets.

Many times a commodity will over run it's value and excessive price will bring an opportunity to make a quick gain in a market correction. Oil in recent years has traded between $11 and $36 a barrel, so if we could have made a trade when the price had overshot it's values, we would have made money.

This happens from time to time and a trade should only be considered once we are in-tune with the commodity and the supply and demand factors.

High tech stocks are regarded as commodities by some analysts. The way they have traded gives credit to this chain of thought. Once we realize the markets are treating stocks the same as commodities, we can gauge the extent of their exaggerated price.
We now can buy when they are overly cheap and sell when we feel they are overpriced. A feel for commodities gives us an extra feel for trading stock.

Gold has been neglected for the past twenty years. In the early eighties gold traded at $800 an ounce. Today it languishes around $270 ounce. Apart from jewelry and a little industrial demand gold has lost it's glitter.It once was a safe haven for money in times of crisis. The dollar has taken on that role to all intents and purposes. There will come a day when the dollar will weaken and Gold will become a safe haven once more. When will that be? I do not know but keeping a close watch over all commodity prices and world events will sound warning signals, before the herd is alerted. The bible states there are sometimes seven years of plenty, seven years of famine. Gold could one day be a safety net in a famine.

There is an old story about a dog with a bone in his mouth crossing the Bridge. He was in the middle of the bridge when he looked down and noticed another dog with bone in his mouth. Of course it was his refection but he did not know that. The other dogs bone looked much bigger than his, so he opened his mouth to attack the other dog and steal his bone. He dropped his bone in the water and was unable to retrieve it.

Many times in life we look what others possess and do not see what treasures we hold. If we are jealous of other peoples possessions, then no matter how much money we make, we will never be satisfied. Contentment of living with that which we possess, will give us the ability to get what we need.

When it come to stock or commodity brokerage charges we have to be prudent. The definition of the word broker could mean 'poorer that you were before,' if you pay your stock broker large commission fees. Some full commission brokers charge over two hundred dollars per trade. That is over four hundred dollars to buy and sell a stock. If we trade often, we will go broke with all those commissions. Are getting great advice, showing good profits, from our full commission broker?

• There is no sense in paying high commissions if we are

not. Why pay more than necessary?

- What value is there in a good relationship. Good for who?
- How accessible is he/she?

- Can we get through immediately we want to place a trade?
- A few minuets delay can be extremely costly.

- Do we get a good fill once our order has been executed or are we the one that has been decimated with an unfair price?
- Are there any maintenance charges on our account?

The more questions we ask, the more unclouded the answers become.

When we give a market order, we should always repeat it and then ask the broker to repeat it back. Be clear and precise. If we say buy and we meant to say sell it can be a very expensive faux pas. Make sure the broker repeats the order. Once we are given a price of the transaction, this is called the "Fill'

Always ask for the buy and sell spread before giving the order. Sometimes in volatile markets, the difference between the buy and sell price can be huge and it may not be wise to deal at that moment.

When we do deal, take notice of the price we get. If it is lower than the price we were quoted ask the reason why. If it happens more than three times, as to speak with the room supervisor. Ask for the "time of sale" ticket and then we can see how the stock was trading when we gave the order.

Always look at the time, when we give our order. That way it is harder for then to cheat us on the fill. If we are getting too many bad fills, change brokers and report them to the SEC (Securities and exchange Commission.)

If we have a large portfolio an account can be opened whereby we do not pay any commission and we can trade as many times as wish. We just pay one percent of our average portfolio value per year. This is paid quarterly.

If we are making our own trades this is called an unsolicited trade and the commissions should be inexpensive. Some discount brokers charge as low as $5 a trade. The average is around $ 20-$25 a trade with a reliable broker.

Trading on-line is a quick and cheap way to trade stocks but the fills may not be so hot and many on-line accounts do not trade stocks valued below $5 a share.
Real time quotes are a necessity before any deal.

One joy dispels a hundred cares. Confucius

We face many problems in life but when we can laugh at ourselves our biggest problem is solved. M. L.

No 19 Adapt to change. Be flexible

Switching Channels.

Our brain, comparable to a television set, can tune into many different programs. When we were born we received a brain capable of tuning into all the joy in the universe. But then we got distracted by other programs broadcasted by fear and limiting beliefs. Here's a way to reconnect ourselves to Powerful energy.

We get a gift of a brand new Magical TV which has unlimited access to all the beautiful channels. When we tune into any one of the millions of stations we become embraced with wonderful joy filled feelings.

We are given a remote control and can instantly connect to all the marvelous programs at will. We are really enjoying switching channels and experiencing lots of happy days.

Time progresses, and the remote control is not working so well anymore. We can no longer get our favorite channels, and the ones we can get we really do not care for.

A little later, even the programs we tolerate start to get distorted. The signals become weak and there is a lot of interference. The TV has trouble getting enough electric power as the tube is getting worn out, working so hard to connect to even the mediocre stations.

The magic has now gone out of the TV set, and the tube fades away. The power source can no longer travel inside the set, as the receiver has extinguished itself.

Re_tuning our Brain

When we were born we received a brain that was clear and sharp and could tune into all the joy in the universe. It also has the ability to tune into messages of Joy from all it sees, hears, feels, touches and smells.

As we grow and mature control of our awareness, this mechanism starts to disappear and the joy of life slowly fades away. We search desperately for the way we can turn on our joy, but the more effort we put into seeking the joy the more miserable we become.
We question ourselves, doubt ourselves, and even start to hate ourselves. We might try to blame others for our lost joy, but deep inside we know we cannot tune into a really happy life.

We find many substitutes for joy, like buying new clothes or new cars, making tons of money, smoking, drinking alcohol, taking drugs.
We have learnt to tolerate a lifestyle we are not so happy with. But what can we do, it is all most of us have.

In order to enjoy life, we first need to get our mind in order. We have learnt to endure and forgot how to enjoy.
If we realize there is a way to recharge our control of awareness, which will put us in tune with harmony, love, contentment and a true joy of life, we get a second chance.

The receiver in our brains needs to switch on to the correct voltage and allow the currents of intelligent energy to flow through our whole system.

As we re_energize ourselves, we begin to feel real power surges and can tackle any distortion that comes our way. Nothing prevents us from receiving a beautiful clear picture of Health, Wealth, and Happiness. We are tuned into Life is Beautiful, and we do not need to switch channels any more.

By detaching ourselves from the physical world we see around us, and attaching to a power source of intelligence that has created and evolved all life and matter, we find the real way of living as human beings.

We now can enjoy all the physical world has to offer, and also become a creative link in the chain of evolution. We take pleasure in helping our fellow men and women make their life a happy one.

We realize that the pure potential of infinite wisdom is a channel that is linked to our minds, and we have access to it when we clear the way to receive it. We never get sick, never worry and are always contented.

The Magic of Infinite Silence. Does it sound like Magic?

Well it... IS (I. S. = Infinite Silence).

With-In, In-finite Silence we connect with Spirit. It is there that we recharge our batteries on a daily basis. When we feel the Divine Bliss this magic energy gives us, we want to soak up every ounce.
After a while, we find we can connect to this channel day and night. In a crowded room or all alone. We can turn on the power at will. We never feel lonely.

Our freewill is tuned into God because that gives us Joy, not because we are instructed to by religion. We now know what

will power means.
Spirit is directing us, not human rules and regulations.

We now can throw away the remote control. We will never feel remote, alone or far away from Universal intelligence. For we are automatically connected __ 24 hours a day, 7 days a week, 52 weeks a year.
Eventually we will throw away our body and live in eternal, Divine Bliss.

But not just yet. We have a whole lot of programs to really enjoy. We are richer then any millionaire for we possess seven trillion cells in our bodies and twenty billion neurons in our mind. So lets tune in the neurons and start living like a Joy filled billionaire.

 The only thing that holds us back in life are our own thoughts. If we become too rigid, we will eventually snap. Once we reverse the process and become flexible, we will be able to adapt to each situation as it arises.

The More Results one man get's the more Mankind wins. M. L.
Intellect and Intelligence may be close stable mates but one is a Hacker the other a Thoroughbred. M. L.

Good has two meanings: it means both that which is good absolutely and that which is good for somebody.
_ Aristotle

Call on God, but row away from the rocks.
_ Indian Proverb

A pessimist sees the difficulty in every opportunity; an optimist sees the opportunity in every difficulty.

Sir Winston Churchill

God wears a real designer label. M. L.

No 20 We Are Our Own, Number One Asset.

Should we run our own business? If we are worth $50,000 to our boss, we must be worth $100,000 to ourselves. The best investment we can make is, in ourselves.

The very fact we were born means we hit the jackpot. It was a million to one shot for the sperm to hit the egg. We have the chance of a human experience. Everything else is a bonus. The journey of a lifetime starts with the first step. When we were born, we possessed the wisdom of the universe, now we must try and retrace our steps.

Opportunities will come along very often but we must be aware of them. Coca Cola was discovered when a pharmacist spotted two boys drinking his headache syrups. It gave him the notion to make it into a soda. Finding things "by chance" means an open mind seizing the moment. Most good things happen "By chances " or do they?

Could it be the more we enjoy our tasks, the more success will attach itself, with no effort.
If we work twelve hours a day and all twelve hours are enjoyable then it becomes effortless. But if we spend our time watching the clock and can't wait to run to a bar or pub for a beer, we will find life a hard slog. Everywhere we look opportunities abound. A closed shop can only open with the proprietors permission.

If a big recession comes along, there is a probable chance of unemployment, so it is always good to have another string to our bow. The way our mind is conditioned gives us a mental picture of ourselves. These images stay throughout our life unless we take steps to change them. To effect a break though and fracture the mold we have fabricated, we need to begin a new business.

We can start a small internet business, before giving up a job. Don't throw away dirty water, until we find clean. Every day is a fresh opportunity to continue the quest towards our mission of self reliance.

Finding our true self is a lifetimes quest. It can be likened to a golf swing. Just when we think we have got it mastered, it disappear. So it is with our true identity.

How do we know how to access the true self. Well, it takes The three Ps.– One day a Guy is lost in New York and asks a passerby for directions. He asks "How do you get to Carnage Hall" The reply comes back; "Practice, Practice, Practice."

Every day of our lives we need to find time to sit in silence for fifteen minuets. The greatest sages all found the answers to life's enigmas, in the silent zone. Having a clear mind allows fresh thoughts to flow freely.

It is not a case of; is the cup is half full or half empty. It needs to be completely empty, so new and unfamiliar images can filter through ,untainted by the old worn out perceptions.

The other three Ps; Patience, persistence, perseverance are also a necessity for a successful life. We never give up on our dreams, for everything we imagine can become our reality. Realistic images are born in our imagination. When we dream our reality and live our dreams we travel a truly successful path.

A Negative focus.
There once was a monastery that kept very strict rules.

Observing a vow of silence, no one was allowed to speak. There was one exception to this rule. Every ten years, the monks were sanctioned to speak just two words. After playing out his first ten years at the monastery, one monk went to the chief monk. "It has been ten years," said the principal monk. "What are the two words you would like to vocalize.
"Room , Drafty" said the monk.
"I see," replied the head monk.

Ten years later, the monk revisited the dominant monk's office. "It has been ten additional years," said the head monk. "What are the two words you would like to speak?"

"Provisions, Terrible..." said the monk.
"I see," replied the head monk.
Another ten years expired and the monk once again encountered the boss monk who asked, "What are your two words now, after these ten years?"
"I... resign said the monk."Well, I can see why," retorted the leader. "All you ever do is Grumble
Learn the Rules of the game but don't let them become more important than the game itself. M. L.

We should not get too tied down with rule and regulations, don't become ridged. We will face many problems but when we have learnt to laugh at ourselves the biggest problem is solved. Never be envious of others with more money and never let our emotions control our feelings. We will all encounter possible issues we do not care for. It is not the problems, it is how we handle them.

The more wisdom we gain, the smaller the problems become, then they dissipate. Once we walk on a true path, we should not be distracted, by the comments of other people. Many folks are very fickle. One minute they can love us, the next they dislike us. We cannot live our lives by the way others view our

actions, as long as our actions a made with good intent.
First they ignore you,
Then they laugh at you,
Then they fight you,
Then you win. Mahatma Gandi.
Enjoying Each Moment.
Once upon a time there was a golf pro, who closed his golf shop at three o'clock every day and went out to play golf, with his mates or members of the golf club. One day he was playing with a well know billionaire. The guy was spouting off about how successful he had become. He told the pro that he had just retired at the age of seventy five. He asked the pro how old he was. The reply was twenty five. "Now let me tell you young man, that if you work hard for the next fifty years, you will be able to retire a wealthy man just like me."
"What Then?" Asked the young golfer.
Why then you will be able to play golf every afternoon.

Joy. Enjoy your work. More joy, more money.
Wouldn't it be wonderful to go to work each day doing the kind of work that we love to do? Once we have identified our work values, that is exactly what we can do. Often, it is possible to find new ways to use the intelligence we already possess. Once recognized, they may transform the job we are already doing. If not, is it time to start to think about the kind of work, that would give feelings of fulfillment, to the talents we enjoy.

Maybe we can turn a hobby into a business. Enthusiasm is a great motivator for success. Sometimes 'Old Fashioned' sells. Even if we have retired from our regular job does not mean we have retired from life. We need to keep an active mind. We can become a film extra, do charity work or work at the theater as an attendant and get to see all the great shows for free. We can become a golf ranger and take in the great scenery and fresh air. Get out to meet and greet folks.

If we want to make more money, perhaps we can sell our grandpa's old fashioned ice cream, made from family recipes. Look at old books and find old recipes. We can sell home baked cookies and cakes, knitting and quilts, art work and a host of other hobbies. Be a little outrageous. Get free publicity. Do something that will make people sit up and take notice.

We can get our friends and neighbors involved and lead a home industry. We can get affiliates to sell our home made products. There may be snow on the top but there is still fire down below. Keep firing on all cylinders. Good-looking young folks are accidents of nature, But attractive old people are compositions of art.

Things may not always turn out as planned. Sometimes a success comes out of a disaster and a disaster can come out of success. It's not how we start, It's how we finish that counts. Having fun in between, is the most important component of success. Enjoy the journey and don't be in too much of a hurry to get to the destination. Once we propel with enthusiasm, we will win our challenges. Drive with show and put for dough.

It does not matter if we are working for a company or ourselves, we must enjoy the experience. Don't focus only on making money. Forget the numbers and do things for the good of the job in hand. Go the extra mile. Do things from the heart & Soul. Let's distinguish ourselves from other similar products and services.

A thing of beauty is a joy forever:
Its loveliness increases; it will never
Pass into nothingness; but still will keep
A bower quiet for us, and a sleep
Full of sweet dreams, and health,
and quiet breathing.

John Keats,

Have fun making money. Laugh a lot. Keep the atmosphere joyful in the workplace and at home. Play music, dance and sing more often. When we shower in the morning, imagine we are in a waterfall, at some exotic location. Let's use our imagination more. It is our true image maker. If we are stuck in traffic jams, look up at clouds, and see all the different shapes. Stand out at work, make sure the big boss knows who we are.

Most people die with their music still inside them.
Oliver Wendell Holmes

You're never too old to become younger." Mae West

Great minds have purposes, little minds have wishes
 Washington Irving

Our deeds determine us, as much as we determine our deeds._ George Elliot

Each Box .

Each box projects a life behind an illuminated screen,
A myriad of choices, clues to happiness of self-esteem,
Many refreshments of the mind all uniquely locked inside
Savor the various flavors, before the key's of truth turn n
hide.

Each box has numerous secrets wholly tucked away,
Some are endowed treasures 'souly' reserved for a rainy day,
Others are cherished pearls from wisdom's infinite array,
Whilst a few drink nectar from the golden goblet of
Mandalay.

Each box has special switches to turn on spirits light,
It is well hidden, packed away by ego's contorting might,
But when the channels are connected, a powerful candle is lit
The riches of the soul appear, simple; yet incredibly exquisite.

Each box is filled with mystical chocolates, orgasmic to the
taste,
Fed to new born infants but lost in a race with to much haste,
Intelligence tunes in at birth, played on a baby Grand.
How wisdom trickles through, the human grains of sand. M.
L.

No 21 Our credibility is a major asset in the business world.

Always be honest.

We should always admit our ignorance about subjects we don't understand. Don't try to bluff intellects or business folk who have been around for a long time. Never tell lies because when we get found out, folks will lose their respect for us. Remember the old quip, "it's easier to tell the truth, as you won't have to remember, which lies you told, to whom"? A self pretense, is the ultimate lie and in the long run it will hurt the holder most of all.

If we get a promotion at work, we should accept it graciously. If we go around boasting, we will lose respect of others.

A Large Ego Creates a Fool.
A guy comes home from work and tells his wife he has just been made vice president of his brokerage firm. He continues to tell her how great he is all week long. At the end of her patience she explodes. " Well at our office we have a vice president of toilets." He immediately called her bluff and phones up the wife's firm. "Can I speak to the vice president of toilets please? He asked. "Mens or Ladies?" The phone operator replied.

Building up our credibility may take a long time and we should be careful how we approach new situations. If we do things with good intent, then no matter what some folks may say, our intentions of goodness, will override any errors. We should conduct ourselves with consideration for others at all times. Should we ever get a bad reputation for being mean and miserly it will stick like glue.

True story.

There was an old man who had made a fortune but could not bare to spend any of it. He was a friendly chap and was always very polite. Every day he would go to his golf club and enjoy his golf but after the game he would never buy a drink.

He would sit at the table and if someone offered him a cup of tea he would be delighted to accept. Never once did he reciprocate. He also had another very strange habit. He would steal a newspaper. In the afternoon, around four-thirty, he would push a newspaper under his sweater and take it home for his wife to read. Folks could see him do this but nobody ever said anything. When the man died he left many millions of dollars but in reality he died a pauper. Being miserly to ourselves is just as bad as being a spendthrift and always being broke.

Some folks who have come from a poor background find it hard to spend any money and they begrudge themselves the luxuries of life, that they could well afford. We can live a simple life even though we are wealthy but to live as a miser is a sickness of no self worth. We cannot give to others if we cannot treat ourselves with unconditioned love. This is not a selfish love. Rather it is a love that embraces the whole of life with Joy. We need to know ourselves, before we can trust ourselves. Ignorance of our true identity does us much harm.

Hitch your wagon to a star. Let us not fag in paltry works which serve our pot and bag alone. Let us not lie and steal. No god will help. We shall find all their teams going the other way: every god will leave us. Work rather for those

interests which the divinities honor and promote, justice, love, freedom, knowledge, utility. Ralph Waldo Emerson,

WHO CAN WE
T
R
U
S
T

Many plans can be at stake,
On the actions of a mere handshake,
Sometimes we make a great mistake,
For the handshake was a friendly fake.

There are times we trust an honest face,
On their smile is the judgement we base,
We give them credit but alas what a waste,
For they disappear without any trace.

Then we find a partner which we love,
Wooing and cooing as two little doves,
But it soon changes to push and shove,
Love flies out the window, to somewhere up above.

So who can we trust, on what can we rely,
How can we know if we are being told a lie,
To find the truth, we must look through our third eye,
And follow spirits guidance, from a reality upon high.

M. L.

He who has no vision of eternity has no hold on time.
 Thomas Carlyle

No man is rich enough to buy back his past. Oscar Wilde

The higher we are placed, the more humbly we should walk. Cicero

22 Always give more than you take. Help others to run their business.

One of the most basic laws of the universe is Karma. What goes around come around. The more we are able to share our knowledge and know how with others the more we will prosper. Many folks believe giving money is the answer to helping others and while it does alleviate a problem for a short time, it is not a long term solution.

Feeding folks the correct information on how to live a meaningful life is true giving. It will be repaid ten fold in many different ways. And yes, we will receive financial rewards which seem to come **"Out of the Blue"** Those who have read **"Minds of Blue Souls of Gold"** will know what I mean.

When we help others to gain wealth, we gain wealth, as they grow, we grow. Build togetherness with all costumers and suppliers in all our dealings. The more we share, the more we gain.

Story Time.

There once was a great banquet, where all the town's people

were invited. It took place in a big baronial hall. The room was bedecked with an array of banners and colors and wonderful musicians played delightful music. Just one big table stretched round the room. It was covered with all the finest foods and drink from around the world. The succulent foods was plentiful and all the towns folk sat opposite one another.

There was just one major problem. Everyone had a plaster cast on their arms so they could not feed themselves. Their arms could not bend and they had no way of putting food into their own mouths. One wise man stood up, picked up some food and fed the person directly in front of him. Everyone stood up and applauded him and they did the same.

When we take the focus off ourselves and feed others, our wisdom, we progress along our magical pathway to success.

Ancient Story.
 Two monks were sat by a river when they observed a scorpion that was drowning. One monk instantly took it out of the water and put it on the bank. In the process he was stung. A few minutes later the scorpion fell in again. The kindly monk rescued the scorpion and was stung a second time. " my dear one, why do you continue to save the scorpion when you know it's nature is to sting?"The other monk inquired "Because," the monk replied, " It's my nature to save life."
^^^
We can only be true to ourselves, when we truly know ourselves M. L.

There are numerous ways to lose the joy of the day but there are none that will return the day .M.L.

Desire joy and thank God for it. Renounce it, if need be, for other's sake. That's joy beyond joy.
 Robert Browning

What I kept, I lost; What I spent, I had; What I gave, I have. _ Persian Proverb

The best way to get even is to forget. _ Anonymous

He who forgives ends a quarrel. _ African Proverb

Each hour of each day is a blessing. When we pass our Joy on to others we are fulfilling our authentic purpose. We are timeless beings wrapped in a Finite Time Zone. When we Pull back, detach from all we know we will start to discover peace. In the silence of our tranquil mind we will flow with the pure potential of Spirit. We will then find we have the fortitude and energy to face life's lessons in a more meaningful way.
I Am The One.

I am the discreet whispers on the breeze.
Listen to my voice as it brushes your delicate cheek,
I am all you think - all you seem - all you contemplate,
My thoughts are etched in every rock

Through eons of years I have called your name,
No replies have been heard, no true purpose found,
Listen to my voice as it sails upon the wind,
You need to know my message - to find authentic meaning.

As I float on by your mind - be aware,
You know I am around you,
Yet you will not listen to my voice
Could it be your choice is not of your choosing?

I am your own true self dear one,
I have been here forever and a day,

Will you suffer in your illusion - endure rather than enjoy,
Or will you becalm your mind -become aware of my timeless
silent voice,
^^^^^^^^^^^^^^^^^^^^^^^^^^^^^^^^^^

**Every day is a Holy-day and we turn it into a Holiday for
the celebration of life. Enjoy every second on this precious
paradise called Earth. M. L.**
**Look and you will find it_what is unsought will go
undetected._ Sophocles**
We never compete, we Lead.

If we think of all the competition that we could face in our lives
and the business world, it could deter our plans. We may be
disheartened and discouraged from trying anything new if we
believe we have to compete with powerful opposition.
We need to realize, they are who they are - we are who we are.
We have no need to prove anything to anybody. We set out on
our own course - chart our own route. Then we set sail and let
Spirit chose the degrees. Allow others follow if they wish. The
more success we achieve, the more others will follow. If we
start out as a leader, we will finish as a leader. If we start out as
a follower, we may never finish.

We will find we can magnetize folks into our live so we all
prosper together. Success breeds success therefore once we
develop a positive attitude - we will fly to higher altitudes.

learning to use all the new ideas the high tech world provides
makes our venture easier. Information technology is the way to
improve our capability to progress swiftly. We become
conversant with everyone else's methods and we learn to do
efficiently. The more we ask questions, the more we learn from
other commercial masters in our chosen field of undertakings.
We broaden our horizons and learn skills at all levels; Law,
accountancy, property. etc

- We read balance sheets of similar companies. We observe their profit margins so that we can cut our expenses and expand our sales.

- We price products competitively and keep up to date with trends.

- We Project solid cash flow.

- We train our staff to be and give their best at all times.

- We give them a share of the company.

- We remember birthdays and take an interest in their problems to help them achieve their goals.

- We don't Criticize other companies or blame anyone else for our mistakes.

When we point a finger at anyone we find, there are always three more pointing back at us. Try pointing!!!

We should mark our diaries with daily events, to read later. Then we can see what needs to be done, to improve our actions, on an on going basis.
We continue to ask our self, how can we use the values we recognize in our self, to get the best from our time? We make a promise to use our inner treasures of wisdom, in our everyday performance on the world stage.
No matter what folks may think about us, we should never be deterred from our focus and fulfillment of living a truly prosperous life.
He who asks is a fool for five minutes, but he who does not ask remains a fool forever. - Chinese proverb

Our World can be textured to be:-
As Rough as hopsack and as coarse as hessian.
            Or:-
As smooth as silk and as soft as satin.
In the fabric of life we weave our own cloth. M. L.

Self importance leads to self impotence. M. L.

There was a lady by the name of **Mother Teresa** who's only possessions was a mop, bucket and a robe. These are her words.

People are often unreasonable, illogical, and self-centered; Forgive them anyway.

If you are kind, People may accuse you of selfish, ulterior motives; Be kind anyway.

If you are successful, you will win some false friends and some true enemies; Succeed anyway.

If you are honest and frank, people may cheat you; Be honest and frank anyway.

What you spend years building, someone could destroy overnight; Build anyway.

If you find serenity and happiness, they may be jealous; Be happy anyway.

The good you do today, people will often forget tomorrow; Do good anyway.

Give the world the best you have, and it may never be enough;
Give the world the best you've got anyway.

You see, in the final analysis, it is between you and God;
It was never between you and them anyway.

Mother Teresa.

No 23 Property Has been the best investment of All.
Over the years the best investment has been home ownership.
They say a man/woman's home is their castle. The price of a
modest home in a good district in the sixties cost ten thousand
dollars. Today it will be at worth at least two hundred thousand
dollars. This beats any other investment for the average family.

The number one criteria when buying a home is; Location,
Location, Location. Checkout the district before making any
commitments. Go round the district at different times and
check out the neighbors. The last thing we need is to move next
door to the neighbors from Hell. When we find a home we like
take a close look for subsidence . Keep a keen sense of smell to
check for mustiness or damp. Check for cracks near window
frames and doorways. If there is new plaster and paint,
investigate a little closer, all around that area.

Be carful not to buy at peak times, if we are not selling our own
house simultaneously at the peak. Many first time buyers can
be caught out by purchasing when prices are too high. They
may be left with a negative mortgage, which means they are
paying for a property that has decreased in value and the
mortgage is more than the property is worth. If prices are sky
high and the gut feeling is to holdout from purchasing, then it
might be a good idea to rent for a short while whilst prices
stabilize.

Time share property is not a good investment. It makes more sense to rent a property for holidays or buy one with a group of friends or relatives if we wish to share. It will work out much cheaper and will appreciate in value.

When we invest in commercial properties, the number one criteria is the same as when we buy our home, Location, Location, Location. We must always guard against uncertain events. Assets turn to liabilities when they start to depreciate in value. Losing money can be limited if we protect our vulnerability.

We should not purchase commercial property when prices are high and the economy is booming. That is a great time to Sell. When the building is full of tenants and rents are high. That is when we will get top dollar for our property.

The time to buy commercial property is towards the end of a recession, when the building is empty and has a large liability in property taxes expenses. We can almost name our own price. We still need to know the building is well maintained and no big surprises are in store. If the building has been used by a chemical company, it may have a big liability in cleaning up the ground. If we can relocate our existing business into part of our newly purchased investment property, so much the better.

- Buying property to rent can be a rewarding investment.
- Think of buying-to-let as a medium to long term investment.
- Seek advice from a local letting agents on local market demands but also verify it for ourselves.
- Estimate whether the rent will cover any loans, costs and allowing for vacant periods
- Decorate and furnish to high standards, to attract the

best tenants. This applies to all property we buy including our home.
- Try not to buy a property with potential high maintenance.
- Sometimes it may be an advantage to use a respectable management service to look after our rentals. Delegating our time in a more cost effective way pay's big bucks.
- We should do as much Research and paperwork ourselves. Such as; tenancy agreements, notices, condition reports, inventories and other documentation. If we need help, get a trusted lawyer with low costs. Get a quote first. Better still make a friend out of your agent and let him do all the work. Give him more than he would normally get. It pays to share. Most of all, have fun playing our own brand of 'Monopoly.'

As Only Joy Can Do.

As I sit down on the lush green lawn,

Under the Sycamore tree I have a thought,

It goes against all I have been taught,

but it's not so far apart,

From questions without answers,

from humans with no substance - no heart,

From media's with no root - no soul,

from a society buried deep beneath a festering hole.

How and why do we let the days go "bye,"

Without beaming a smile, rippling a laugh ,

Some meaning that's not a stretch out lie,

To play awhile in an entrancing manner,

To dwell in moments of captivating truths

Stretch space- elongate -lengthen - spin out time

As only joy can do.

No 24 Make your money work. Safe investments with the biggest yields. Invest in what you understand.

Look around the district. See the businesses that are thriving and the ones that are not. Investigate new ideas. Become inventive. What produces do we use on a daily basis? What do we consider good value when we shop?

Values, in this sense, are empowering in finding companies in which to invest our money. If we and others are pleased with the products we are purchasing, then the facts of commerce signifies these values will endure over a given time period.

Buy the product, enjoy the product, then buy the company if it stock price represents value.

Keep a watchful eye out for any new company that you may think there turn in popularity is about to blossom. If we can find a company to invest in before they go public it will reap very rich rewards. **Potential Values** can be enormous and we may spot something in a company the management have overlooked. We could take a more active role as a consultant or director.

From small acorns large oak trees grow.

Form an investment club with friends and neighbors. Discuss strategies. Have a five to ten year time horizon to compound the gains. Figure a time period when you want to retire. Work out how much we will make with a 8% and a 12% return over that period; compounded.

Our money will double every 6-8 years. If our time horizon is 30 years, our money will double nearly five times. A Steady return requires a disciplined approach. If we want to buy Treasury bills we can go directly to Uncle Sam and save between $36 and $60 in transaction fees from brokers and banks.

If we have a lot of money to spare , we could become an Angel. An angel is the term given to a person who invests money in a show or movie. Do it for the fun of it. Not all investment will make money. Most fail to make any decent return therefore only high risk capital should be used. We could hit a winner. An early investment made with Andrew Lloyd Webber and The Really Useful Co. would have made a significant return. But most time 'the fun' of being an angel outweighs the profit equation. We get to meet the stars and can feel part of the production.

"Only those who are prepared to fail greatly can achieve greatly" J F K

Blessed is the man who is too busy to worry in the daytime and too sleepy to worry at night.
_ Anonymous

We may live in a palace or a tent but a cloudy mind will dwell in bad weather.

When we cover our home with a canopy of Joy, we will find beauty in the Storm. M.L.

Sometimes It Takes A Lifetime

Sometimes it takes a lifetime to learn a lesson well,

Angers fester dis_ease because the dogmas so compel,

Doctrines lead up the garden path, as more worries creep,

And in the end, we leave all possessions, outside deaths sleep.

If we stop along the way and start to retrace our steps,

We might find a few clues hidden within the minds depths,

What feels good, what's bad, what make's us ache and yearn,

Who is our master of our fate, why is destiny so stern.

The sooner we come to realize nobody has any control,

In the true forces of spirit that guides the fishes shoal,

To connect to the magic magnetism that makes a human whole,

Surrender the egos might, into the arms of a loving Soul.

No 25 Estate and Asset Planning

It is quite easy to perform a chronicle of our own estate planning and save a sizeable amount of money.

We need to make a list all our possessions - car, boat. jewels, collections, furniture, home business interests, 401 k, possible future inheritance, stock and bonds etc. We should get all our assets, updated with a current valuation. We might have a hidden treasure that is worth many thousands of dollars. If we own an old painting that has been in the family for many years, it could have extended it's value from a few hundred dollars, to hundreds of thousands of dollars.

This may mean a big insurance premium. It could also signify we have an expensive asset but it is a liability to keep it. If we have to pay out big premiums and protect it from being stolen, we have turned an asset into a liability. The best solution is to sell it in an auction, unless we are attached to it and can afford the premiums..

Dealing with Estate planning, wills and taxes, takes planning well ahead of our demise. We need to prepare for uncertainties and eventualities before they happen i.e; loss of a breadwinner, sickness, disablement or accidents.

Probate administration and final expenses costs between 3-5%. Income tax on pensions and annuities could cost up to 39%. Estate tax top rate is 55% so it does not pay to die to soon.

Best to keep ourselves fit and retain a clear mind. Being free of worry and anxiety, is the best prescription. Planning well ahead will save the loved one's a big headache.

If we are married we need advice about being a joint owners or a tenancy in common. There is a big difference. In Joint ownership both parties own all assets. In tenants in common each person owns one half of the assets. This could have serious tax implications. Asset allocation can be worked out within a given time horizon.

There are Living trusts, either Revocable- Irrevocable. We also need an executor, a trustee, and of course the beneficiary. Keep it all very simple. Don't go into complicated plans that may save money down the line and cost a lot to set up now. Legislation is changing and what is relevant now, will have no significance in a few years time. So don't pay out expensive fees. Make a simple will or trust fund.

Take care of funeral and burial expenses. When we proceed to make our wills, trusts and annuities, make sure all our family know about our assets and where they are. If we pop off in some distant land, whilst enjoying a world cruise, our next of kin may miss out. If we are hoarding some treasures in a hiding place at home, make sure we tell our loved one's where they are.

Many times when we visit a financial adviser or estate planner they will try to sell us a variable annuities

These are tax deferred Mutual funds. They have high management costs and need very careful investigation. Take time in coming to any final decision. Remember to 'look before you leap'

Many folks move or die and the accounts are forgotten. The state claims them after two years. It is called escheated. Many banks may have amounts as much as three hundred million dollars or more in unclaimed accounts.

New York has 4 billion in unclaimed property. Have you got a distant relative that passed away years ago, in a far away state or county? You might have a pot of gold somewhere

Check safe deposits in banks of the dearly departed. It my cost us dear if we don't. Take a look at 'missingmoney.com'

or check within the state of your distant relative.

Keep an active mind. Handle your stress levels, eat healthy food, exercise and you will live to one hundred years of age. You will outshine any billionaire if you stay fit and contented.

But in this world nothing can be said to be certain, except death and taxes. Benjamin Franklin,

Just one more thought. If we have aged parents, look after them, after all we will be old one day.

Ancient Story.

A kindly farmer got so old and fatigued that he could no longer work. So he would pass the day just sitting on his rocking chair on the porch. His son, working hard on the farm, would observe his father sitting there and it really bugged him. "He's of no use any more, and he does nothing but lounge around. I am tired of supporting him!" He thought.

Feeling frustrated y the son built a good-looking wooden coffin, and told his father to jump in. Without consider the consequences the father laid down inside. On shutting the lid, the ungrateful son hauled the coffin to the edge of a high cliff. As he came to the edge, his old kindly dad started a light tapping sound from inside the coffin. He opened it up.

Lying inside quite and peacefully, the father looked up at his ungrateful son. "I know you are going to throw me over the cliff, but before you do, may I suggest something?"

"If you must, but it will not make any difference" replied the son.

"Throw me over the cliff, if it will make you feel superior" uttered his old dad, "but save this coffin made of such beautiful wood . Your children might need to use it one day"

Death is the doorway to everlasting joy. If we live as a true soul here on earth, we will not even differentiate the

distinction between life and death, for in reality a soul cannot die. When we live as a true soul, we live in joy.

Life is thickly sown with thorns, and I know no other remedy than to pass quickly through them.
The longer we dwell on our misfortunes, the greater is their power to harm us. Voltaire .

If there is no wind, row. _ Latin Proverb

Turn your face to the sun and the shadows fall behind you. _ Maori proverb

Words must be weighed, not counted. _ Polish Proverb

You can't wake a person who is pretending to be asleep. _ Navajo Proverb

We abide in an enchanted forest. Our path has been carved by the divine. We have a choice; we can follow the path of enlightenment whereby we will find all the beauty this human existence has to offer, or we can use our minds as a machete and hack our way through the undergrowth of egos and make our own path. By following this route we will soon become tired, weary and lost in a jungle of materialistic confusion.

We are now aware we have a magical path to follow. The divine is in all of life. With our eyes open or closed. Awake or in slumber, we live in the peaceful Forrest of the Mind.

PEACEFUL SLUMBER IN THE FOREST OF THE MIND.

Listen! How sweet sings the breeze, merrily off trees, whispering wonderment, the ear quietly it does please, nurturing souls, drifting to Celestial splendor, beauty unfolds, as into peaceful slumber, coils surrender.

Castles in the sky, growing columns of inspired aspiration, silver shadows flowing through all generations, warm cocoons of mortality, linked by silken threads, webs of lives where comfort embeds.

Serenely rests the head of time, pillows puff by wisps of the sublime, mellow moments spark a fusion sphere, perfumed gardens alight, dancing nymphs are near.

Oh mindful forest flower, rivers many bridges cross, branches leaved with neurons, invisible flakes of frost, tender is the night, spirits lovingly caress, sleep well my children, aware God will bless.

No 26 Keep Healthy if you are sick you can't earn money.

We will have gathered by now that there is much more to living a life of wealth than meets the eye. We need universal wisdom to ensure a successful, healthy, fun loving life of infinite style and possibilities. We must invest in our heath, for if we get sick, all the money in the world will not help to regain lost energy.

A Feast for the Senses.

Our health is more precious than any diamond and yet we allow it to deteriorate out of ignorance of True information and attach our thoughts to misinformation. We know smoking and drinking alcohol is a quick way to a hospital bed but still many folks say this is what they enjoy. New scientific evidence is educating us to the fact eating: meat, dairy, candies, chocolate, cookies, cakes, sodas and foods containing hydrogenated fats and artificial flavors may lead to illnesses such as cancer and heart attacks.

The foods we are eating, eats away at our life span.

Most of us know fresh fruit, vegetables, whole grains, nuts, etc. should be our wholesome diet. But we keep eating the toxic food until we make ourselves ill and die too soon.

They say we are what we eat. In truth we are what we think.

The question then becomes: Who is directing us to eat all the wrong foods and why do we continue to do so even when we now know it is shortening our life? Our perception of living a happy life has been built with a good education but little wisdom.
If we are treating our bodies in this manner it is quite likely we are treating our minds in the same way. It is quite possible that negative thoughts have a knock on effect and make us look for a substitution for happiness.
We are wined and dined with a mass of information on the negative side of life. We bear a grudge, we seek revenge, we are resentful, we worry and become anxious, we hold fear and hatred. Frustrations and devastations pile on the agony. We feed ourselves a banquet of negative toxic thoughts. This is all stored in our memories and seeps into our conscious minds on a daily basis. We have allowed people & events we have no

control over in this world to control our minds. On top of all this we also have the media to contend with.

We allow the advertising media to brainwash us into thinking we desire certain tastes and this will bring us Joy. We sample the goods and they taste real good.

We now educate our subconscious to trigger a desire of harmful but tasty food whenever we have a negative thought. This is done automatically and the desire takes on its own momentum so we get cravings for unhealthy food most of the time. Our body's tell our minds to crave tasty types of food. It just becomes routine and "Normal" to eat all the unhealthy foods and when someone comes along to advise on a healthier way of eating they are called a crank and dismissed from our minds.

Then one day we become sick, we take many types of medication and it may relieve the symptoms for a while but negative thoughts persist. We now become sick from the side effects of the medication on top of the toxic thoughts.
What a concoction of poison we have found for ourselves.

Our minds & bodies have a great defense system and some people can take more stress than others, so there will always be a few people that can abuse their bodies and seemingly get away with it. They really don't. They just have a higher pain threshold and strong Genes. But the majority of folks crack under the stresses and strains of unhealthy living.
I began by saying Our health is more precious than any diamond and yet we allow it to deteriorate out of ignorance of information. So what is the information we need to keep the healthy mind & body most of us were born with.

Every cell in our bodies has been coded over millions of years of evolution and is programmed to think for itself. Our main powerhouse is our brain and the neuron receptors are connected to every cell in our bodies. Our eating habits reflect our thinking therefore We are what we think and take shape from what we eat. The Intelligence that coded our bodies in the first place, is available to guide us throughout our lives. Our pure potential of awareness is called our soul and is a part of Spirit that lodges in our bodies whilst we have a physical presence here on Earth. When we clear our minds we listen to our Soul. The Unified Force Field of Universal Intelligence (God) is our true identity and when we listen to our true selves Health Wealth & Happiness is our reward.

We find we need no reason to be happy.

Joy becomes a state of being.

Joy heals wounds and repairs bodies.

JOY means Just Obey Yourself.

Your true self is a part of GOD.

Now we are fed on SOUL FOOD.

A FEAST FOR THE SENSES.

I do not know what I may appear to the world, but to myself I seem to have been only like a boy playing on the seashore, and diverting myself in now and then finding a smoother pebble or a prettier shell than ordinary, whilst the great ocean of truth lay all undiscovered before me. Isaac Newton

Time is our most precious asset, we should invest it wisely. When we deposit our thoughts in Spirits Irrevocable Trust, we can then bank on Many Happy Returns. M. L 27 Reaping The Rewards From Our Investment Genius.

We have explored many ways to shape an affluent, wholesome life. There may still be some doubt about sustaining our happiness with all the turmoil in the world today. Why do human beings find it so hard to preserve a joyful frame of mind every second of their lives?

Many folks will reply 'It is impossible to feel joy all the time."
Sure enough there are many actions, events, and devastations,
that come into everyone's life at some time or other. It could be
the death of a loved one, a financial failure, a war, terrorists,
chronic illness and many other catastrophic episodes. Some
lead to our demise, some we recover from.

Numerous, everyday occurrence can plague our joy. Arguments
and fights pursue our concepts and beliefs. Events may not
proceed as we planed them. Infidelities, betrayals, stabs in the
back by 'Friends' arise. Stock market gyrations churn the
stomach. We also get weigh down by the problems of other
folks we know. And if all this is no enough we have the media
hurling sensationalistic negative news items at us, from the four
corners of the world.

If we do manage to get a few moments of peace and quite and
relax into a joyful mode, we are hit with advertisements of new
items and goods that we must obtain to keep happy. So our
mind is now transferred to ways of making more money to
acquire things that will only bring fleeting happiness. Many
times we will get into debt to acquire merchandise that we
'Must have.' Acquiring possessions can be fun but they are the
icing on the cake. They are not the cake itself.

After a while of living in a manner which is devoid of any real
joy, we start to feel the effects of living in a stressful
environment. We develop an illness from all our ill-thoughts.
Do you see what is going on here? Are you comprehending
how we have been taken down the garden path to find a rubbish
tip? You see most of the stuff we encounter has no connection
to real Joy.

Once we uncouple our minds from the source of Joy, we
become attached to a transitory, finite world that has no lasting
meaning.

It all seems real enough and nearly everyone one we know embraces it as their truthful world, so who are we to be different? How can we ignore all the 'serious stuff' that everyone one tells us is so important. After all we do not want to be labeled as someone who is uncaring and selfish. What a quandary?

Let's step back a little for a moment. When we were babies, we only knew joy.

We did not hate, we had to grow up first.

We developed a point of view that was handed to us by all the folks we came in contact with. What choices did we have? Could we pick our parents? Could we choose our religion? Did we select our teachers? No, we hade no choice. And now we find ourselves living a life which has very little meaning because we can't find a way to be happy all the time.

So the folks who say it is impossible to be happy all the time are one hundred percent correct. It is impossible to be happy twenty four hours a day, if we subscribe to an unreal superficial world. You see Joy is Real and reality does not mix well with illusions.

'Joy' feels no comfort dwelling in a conceptual world. All we have in a materialistic world is a concept of 'Things' to make us happy and they never can, not in the real sense of happiness. Joy means Just Obey Yourself, your true authentic self.

Not the image of who we think we are, for that was not of our choosing. The reference point that we cling to will only bring anguish and suffering because events happen we have no control over and our reference points are attached to those happening. Real means lasting and nothing in the finite world lasts.

"No Matter What No Matter Lasts."

Therefore why not make our reference point a genuine identity that does last. What is it? It is Joy filled soul, for that is our true authentic identity. It is a oneness, a sameness, a wholeness, a unity, totally in harmony with all the truly exists. Solid with an infinite foundation. Complete, unbounded, unequivocally without borders, labels, banners or divisions. A True genius.

A free flowing essence of pure magical bliss.
This is who we are, our truth. Our Soul. How can we not live in joy every second of every day once we become aware of who we are?

It is impossible not to live in Joy, for Joy-Soul is who we are. Our authentic self. We are the genius within.
No matter what comes along, Joy will endlessly, continuously, ceaselessly, forever, eternally, always be around. Joy is a genius. It's wisdom is indisputable.

Let us now start to acknowledge and recognize our authentic selves. Let us get back to our central position in the Cosmos and balance out thoughts. We find we are directed to health, wealth and true happiness. We make great investments and financial deals for our genius is shining the light of wisdom on all our actions. We eat healthier for our genius loves to live in a healthy body. Our genius will make us aware of every cell in our bodies and we will tune into their feelings. Our genius only knows Joy and once we let the wizard free our lives will be lived in love & joy.
The melodies of the soul are flowing through our mind and body. We radiate the white light of wisdom in a multitude of brilliant color. The maestro is conducing our progress. The orchestrations have all been arranged. Lets dance our mystical waltz in tune to the universal flow. We have returned to paradise and the Garden of Eden has opened it's gates once again. We are invested in our genius and what wonderful treasures we embrace.

When the clock stops ticking and time itself comes to a close, our true essence will still be in JOY. We will know that our investment with our genius, really paid big rewards.

Spirit gave us life and the ability to enjoy everything.
One day we asked Spirit to answer our prayers.
The divine replied: I have provided you with everything.
M. L.

We are all granted the miracle of life and that Joy is enough to take us through life no Matter what obstacles are placed in our way. Just to breath in the air, to feel the breeze brush against our cheek is Magic enough. Each moment should be lived as though it is our last moment on Earth. The field of infinite possibilities is open and our potential pure.

A HAPPY HOBBY HORSE

Lets raise our glasses and make a toast, To a simple pastime we embrace the most, Joy is our hobby, what a powerful force, Entering the human race as a happy hobby horse.

Contentment of living should never be a wager, Keep a steady pace, don't become a galloping major, Jockeying for position could make us interfere, In the celebration of life which we all hold so dear.

Steering our course on the right track, Reining in the anxiety that sometimes does attack, A smile on our face we'll be in the frame, A photo finish winner, more happiness will be our gain.

Every moment, a pleasure, no whip to crack, With love on our saddle there is no looking back, Cantering up the straight, gifts of wonderment unfold, Jumping over hurdles, lead by a soul of gold.

We are each a cell in a Universal body and together we can light up the Cosmos. M. L.

　　　　　　　　　　　　　　　　(

www.ingramcontent.com/pod-product-compliance
Lightning Source LLC
Chambersburg PA
CBHW021419210526
45463CB00001B/455

* 9 781797 485126 *